EFFECTIVE TOP MANAGEMENT TEAM
AN INTERNATIONAL PERSPECT"

COI

Please

"I would strongly recommend this book to every manager who is – or who aims to become – part of the top managerial rank in their organisation. It brings out the difficult dilemmas involved in building top management teams and provides practical advice on how to approach them."

Kieran Mc Gowan, Chairman, Irish Management Institute
and Director of several companies.

"This book provides a comprehensive, cutting-edge and detailed review of the top management team literature. It should be required reading for all doctoral students in strategic management and for researchers interested in advancing our understanding of how top management teams impact organizational outcomes. The book is organized in a manner that makes the complex ideas and theories 'come alive' with importance. I highly recommend it!"

Ken G. Smith, Robert H. Smith School of Business,
University of Maryland.

"For twenty years I have consulted with, debated with, worked with the top groups of private and public organisations in various countries. In all that time I knew that there was a direct relationship between how that group performed as a team and the performance of that organisation. Proving that relationship to be true has been elusive. Knowing it to be true, having worked with hundreds of top teams, has not been a problem. In an applied and easy to read book, the authors have done us all a service. They have gathered together the empirical research, the persistent models and tested techniques to provide CEOs, students, managers and consultants with a first class document.

I recommend it strongly to any manager but particularly to CEOs wanting to know what team building at the top is all about."

John W. Hunt, Professor of Organisational Behaviour,
London Business School.

"This book is a most interesting and thought provoking work, striking a nice balance between the theoretical models and their use in practical situations. The style is clear and crisp. The content covers the key issues impacting on the effectiveness of top teams in a comprehensive, informative and usable manner."

Niall Saul, Group Head of Human Resources,
Irish Life and Permanent, PLC.

"Without a coherent and cohesive top team the probability of organisation change being successful is significantly reduced. Change management consultants gain the confidence and buy-in of chief executives and directors with their understanding of the issues and clear practical interventions and programmes that produce measurable results based on that understanding.

To be effective the change management consultant needs to be on top of the latest research, ideas and methods. I recommend this work for all consultants whose effectiveness relies on challenging, guiding and developing top teams."

Jon Clark, Senior Consultant, Human Capital, Deloitte & Touche.

"*Effective Top Management Teams*, is an invaluable contribution to the latest management thinking and is particularly relevant to School Boards of Management, who are in the process of trying to bring about a culture of team-working at senior management level in a hitherto top-down school system. The development of a holistic education, where pupils are equipped to enter rapidly changing work situations can only be done effectively when team-working is practiced and is evident throughout schools – this book gives clear, practical guidelines on building and working effectively with top teams."

Marian Heeney, Principal & Secretary Board of Management, Presentation School, Wexford.

EFFECTIVE TOP MANAGEMENT TEAMS:
AN INTERNATIONAL PERSPECTIVE

Patrick C Flood
Irish Management Institute and University of Limerick

Sarah MacCurtain
University of Limerick

Michael A West
Aston Business School

BLACKHALL
Publishing

This book was typeset by
Gough Typesetting Services for

BLACKHALL PUBLISHING
8 Priory Hall
Stillorgan
Co Dublin
Ireland
and
BLACKHALL PUBLISHING
2025 Hyperion Avenue
Los Angeles
CA 90027
USA

e-mail: blackhall@eircom.net
www.blackhallpublishing.com

ISBN: 1 842180 17 7

A catalogue record for this book is available from the British Library.

Printed in Ireland by
ColourBooks Ltd

Preface

This book has been researched and written as part of the very productive joint research programme which was launched three years ago between the Irish Management Institute (IMI) and the College of Business, University of Limerick under the joint leadership of Tony Dromgoole, IMI and Patrick Flood, University of Limerick.

The top management group is at the centre of the survival, growth and development of organisations. Sometimes the group operates as a collection of powerful individuals. More rarely, the group bonds together as a powerful and ambitious team, energised by a common vision of what can be achieved. In his important book *The Wealth Creators* published in the early 90's, Andrew Kakabadse found that more than 50% of chairmen and CEO's in Britain and Ireland are concerned about the effectiveness of their top management groups. The book that Patrick Flood and his colleagues have written is therefore of strategic interest to the people who lead and who work in organisations.

This book presents an excellent summary of best practice thinking in this key area and goes on to relate this thinking to our local environment through the research and teaching activities of the authors.

We recommend the book to all chief executives and senior managers who are at the cutting edge of management practice, and to the academics and management development practitioners who are helping to develop the next generation of business leaders.

It is good to see the fruits of co-operation between the IMI and the University of Limerick continuing to emerge. This latest book is an excellent addition to the body of knowledge for both academics and practising managers, and to all of us who work for organisations, which are, themselves, evolving rapidly as the new economy emerges.

Noel Whelan   Barry Kenny
Vice President and Dean,   Chief Executive, IMI
University of Limerick

November 2000

Dedication

We dedicate this book to our families and friends

Patricia, Christopher and Patrick Ellis Flood

For Pat and Mick MacCurtain and Daragh

For Gillian, Eleanor, Nik, Rosa and Thomas

About the Authors

Patrick Flood is Professor of Organisational Behaviour in the College of Business, University of Limerick where he directs the joint IMI–University of Limerick research programmes. Previous appointments include EU Post Doctoral Fellow at London Business School, Fulbright scholar at the R. H. Smith School of Business, University of Maryland at College Park and British Council scholar at the London School of Economics. An alumnus of the International Teachers Programme (ITP), he has taught on many executive education programmes in Ireland, the UK and the USA, specialising in strategic human resource management, leadership and change management. Dr Flood has co-authored or edited several books including *Managing Strategy Implementation* (Blackwell, 2000); *Attracting and Retaining Knowledge Employees* (Blackhall Publishing, 2000); *Managing Without Traditional Methods* (Addison Wesley, 1996). He has published in academic journals such as *Strategic Management Journal*, *European Journal of Work and Organizational Psychology* and *British Journal of Industrial Relations*. A member of the editorial board of *Business Strategy Review*, published by London Business School, he also co-edits *Irish Business and Administrative Research*. Current research interests include the management of knowledge workers; intellectual capital; top management teams; and the business performance effects of strategic human resource management.

Sarah MacCurtain teaches courses on organisational behaviour and human resource management at the College of Business, University of Limerick. She is currently a member of a large research team investigating top team composition, conflict patterns, emotionality and top team performance. Sarah was involved in the PriceWaterhouse Cranfield research project between 1997-1998 exploring the differences in human resource strategies over the last five years in Greenfield sites. She has worked on a consultative basis with several Irish and multinational firms. Sarah is a qualified user of the Myers-Briggs Type Indicator. She is currently a registered doctorate student with Aston University Business School.

Michael West is Professor of Organisational Psychology at the University of Aston Business School. He has been co-Director of the Corporate Performance Programme of the Centre for Economic Performance at the London School of Economics since 1991. He has authored, edited or co-edited twelve books including, *Effective Teamwork, Developing Creativity in Organizations* (BPS,

1997) and the *Handbook of Workgroup Psychology* (Wiley, 1996). He has also written more than 120 articles for scientific and practitioner publications, and chapters in scholarly books. He is a Fellow of the British Psychological Society, the American Psychological Association (APA), the APA Society for Industrial/Organizational Psychology and the Royal Society for the Encouragement of Arts, Manufactures and Commerce. His areas of research interest are team and organisational innovation and effectiveness, and the organisation of national health services.

CONTACT DETAILS:

Professor Patrick Flood,
College of Business,
University of Limerick,
National Technological Park,
Plassey,
Limerick,
Ireland.
Tel: +353-61-202929
Fax: +353-61-330316
EMail: patrick.flood@ul.ie

Sarah MacCurtain,
Dept. of Personnel and
Employment Relations,
University of Limerick,
National Technological Park,
Plassey,
Limerick,
Ireland.
Tel: +353-61-213490
Fax: +353-61-330316
EMail: sarah.maccurtain@ul.ie

Professor Michael West,
Aston Business School,
Aston University,
Birmingham, B4 7ET.
Tel: 0121 359 3611
Fax: 0121 359 2919
EMail: m.a.west@aston.ac.uk

Acknowledgements

Much of the material developed in this book started out as a series of lectures to the students on the Corporate MBA programme at the University of Limerick taking the core course on organisational behaviour taught by Patrick Flood and Sarah MacCurtain. We wish to thank the various cohorts of participants on that programme and in particular the classes of 1998-2000, who, through classroom discussion and debate, have helped to sharpen our ideas and insights into the dynamics of top management teams. Our goal in this book is to bridge the academic treatment of top management teams with the world of the manager. In doing so we have endeavoured to provide some guidelines for the CEO and senior managers charged with the daunting task of building a high performing top management team and crafting strategy. We expect that the contents will be of interest not only to managers but also to academics and executive educators engaged in management development. We hope that it will also encourage further research on corporate performance informed by an upper echelons perspective.

All of the authors have been engaged in long-term programmatic research on top management teams variously conducted at the Irish Management Institute, University of Limerick, London Business School, Aston Business School, the ESRC Centre for Economic Performance at the London School of Economics and the R.H. Smith School of Business, University of Maryland at College Park. We are currently involved in a major study of social and intellectual capital in top management teams conducted under the auspices of the joint IMI/University of Limerick research programme on strategic leadership in association with the R.H. Smith School of Business, University of Maryland at College Park.

In particular we would like to thank our colleagues at IMI, University of Limerick and the University of Maryland at College Park who have helped in various ways including encouraging our research, commenting on draft chapters and sharing their knowledge concerning top management teams. These include Barry Kenny, Tony Dromgoole, Fergus Barry, Charles Carroll, Mike Fiszer, Ruairi O'Flynn and Michael Shiel at IMI; Noel Whelan, Joe Wallace, Margaret Heffernan, Phillip O'Regan, Sarah Moore, Michael Morley, Thomas Turner, Micheál Ó Súilleabháin, David O'Donnell, Teresa O'Hara and Jennifer Farrell, University of Limerick; John Saunders and Jeremy Dawson at Aston Business School; Ken G Smith, Judy Olian, Steve Carroll, Marty Gannon, H P Sims, Kevin Clark, Chris Collins, Cindy Stevens and Don Knight at the University of Maryland. A special word of thanks is due to Ruth Garvey, our editor at Blackhall for his patience and encouragement and to Gerard O'Connor and Tony Mason.

The financial assistance of the Irish Management Institute and the University of Limerick Foundation is gratefully acknowledged for the various research projects reported in this book.

We also wish to thank the many practitioners in the field who have provided us with many invaluable insights and in particular, Pat Cuneen at Analog Devices. Finally and most importantly, Sarah MacCurtain deserves a special mention for her huge contribution to the writing of this book.

We hope that you, the reader, will gain some benefit or insights from this book and encourage you to send comments to the authors at the following email addresses: patrick.flood@ul.ie; sarah.maccurtain@ul.ie; m.a.west@aston.ac.uk. All errors of fact and interpretation are our sole responsibility and we ask readers to bring them to our attention.

On behalf of the Author Team
Patrick C Flood

Table of Contents

List of Figures

List of Tables

Chapter 1

Is the Term "Top Management Team" Appropriate?

INTRODUCTION

The expression "top management team" (TMT) is so often used that it has become, in some situations, little more than an empty term. The word "team" is frequently used to describe groups of individuals who are, in reality, not teams at all. This is especially true when discussing top teams. Hambrick has exposed the fallacy that is so often behind the top team metaphor, stating that "many top management teams have little teamness about them" and are often no more than a collection of people working individually.[1] The question we must ask ourselves is whether the team metaphor is suitable at all for describing the group of individuals who occupy the upper echelons of the organisation or whether, with some considered, though often difficult changes, a top management group (TMG) can become a high performing top team. In the following chapters, we aim to outline the barriers that prevent groups from achieving synergy and becoming true "teams", and describe methods to increase teamwork at the top.

The collection of individuals who occupy the top managerial ranks of the organisation has been referred to using various different terms – "inner circles", top management groups, "dominant coalition" or top management teams, all terms being used interchangeably.[2] The term we prefer to use initially when describing the inner cabinet which does not operate as a team will be the top management group. Sometimes, the inner cabinet operates in a very team oriented way, i.e. high levels of communication, interdependence, consensus decision making and cohesion. However, clearly, only some top teams operate as "teams" in the truest sense of the word. While we feel "group" is usually a more accurate term to describe the constellation of executives at the top, we view the goal of creating and building teamwork within the top management group as a goal worth striving for. In later chapters, where we use the term "the management team" we are mindful of the fact that creating teamwork at the top is a very difficult process.

Figure 1.1: The Different Dimensions to the Top Management Group

External activities

- Market intelligence

- Aligning strategy and competitive environment

Symbolic world

CEO's and TMT's actions carry symbolic meaning in the organisation and externally

Internal activities

- Strategy formation and implementation

- Creating culture

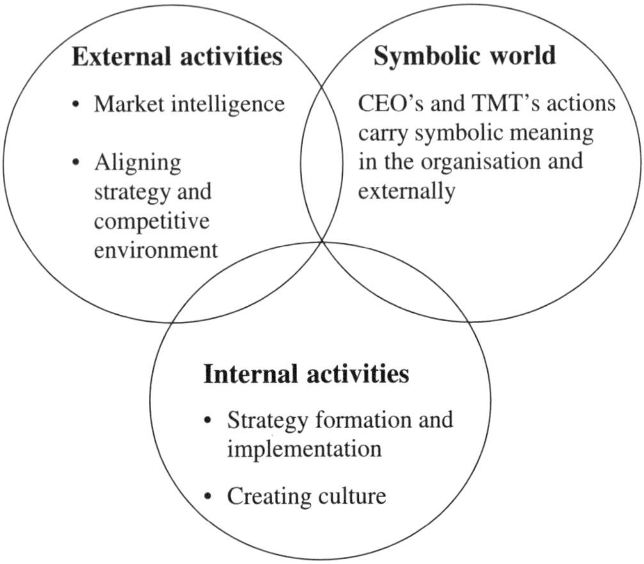

WHY FOCUS ON THE TOP MANAGEMENT TEAM?

Whether the configuration at the top is already an effective team or not, it is important to study such groups as a way of predicting their impact on the organisation. The TMG members operate at the boundary between the external and the internal environment and their organisation. They make the strategic decisions, decisions that are critical to the long-term success of the organisation. Their actions carry high symbolic weight in the organisation as a whole and their influence on corporate culture is pervasive. Research evidence indicates that the TMG, rather than the CEO in isolation, is a better predictor of the organisation's fate.[3] For example, Hage and Dewar established a link between TMG values and the subsequent degree of innovation within the organisation.[4] Halebian and Finkelstein found a positive relationship between the size of the top management groups and company performance, and a negative correlation between CEO dominance and performance.[5]

Organisations are composed of a collection of individuals and groups possessing different goals and agendas, which may come into conflict. The functioning of the TMG, as it comprises the individuals at the strategic summit of the firm, reflects this plurality of goals. How the TMG manages such diversity and inter-functional strains is likely to affect such fundamental organisational outcomes as strategy, structure and performance.

WHAT IS AN EFFECTIVE TEAM?

The transition from group to team is not an easy one. Before going any further, it is first necessary to consider what makes an effective team. Teams, like individuals, have to reflect upon their functioning and adapt in ways which are appropriate to their changing circumstances. Such an orientation requires:

- intelligent scanning of the external environment
- awareness of the functioning of the team and how to manage the team
- flexibility or readiness to change
- the management of paradox
- tolerance of ambiguity and difference within the team
- an ability to accept uncertainty as change occurs.

One reason why simple prescriptions cannot be offered for effective teamwork at the top is that teams operate in varied organisational settings as diverse as multi-national oil companies, voluntary organisations, health care organisations and religious institutions. While top team effectiveness is an important issue in all, the people who constitute these teams are likely to differ in personality, background, industry, experience and education levels and the industry context will reward some attributes of the top management group more than others.

As teams become more diverse in their constitution and functioning, team members must learn to reflect upon, and intelligently adapt to, their constantly changing circumstances in order to be effective. This is the simple but powerful message of this book for those who wish to develop effective team functioning.

TASK AND SOCIAL ELEMENTS OF TEAM FUNCTIONING

There are two fundamental dimensions of team functioning: the task the team is required to carry out, and the social factors which influence how members experience the team as a social unit. The basic reason for the creation of teams in work organisations is the expectation that they will carry out tasks more effectively than individuals and so further progress towards organisational objectives overall. Consideration of the content of the task, and the strategies and processes employed by team members to carry out that task, is important for understanding how to work in teams. At the same time, teams are composed of people who have a variety of emotional, social and other human needs which the team as a whole can either help to meet or frustrate.

In order to function effectively, team members must actively focus upon their objectives, regularly reviewing ways of achieving them and the team's methods of working, sometimes referred to as its task reflexivity. In order to promote the well-being of its members, the team must also reflect upon the ways in which it provides support to members, how conflicts are resolved and what is the overall social climate of the team – or its "social reflexivity".[6] This refers to the capacity of the team to reflect upon and modify objectives, strategies and processes in relation to its task-functional objectives. Social reflexivity is the existence of interpersonal relationships (for example relationships founded on safety, trust, openness and so on) within the group to facilitate such review or reflexive processes. The purpose of these review processes should be to provide active steps to change the team's objectives, ways of working or social functioning, in order to promote effectiveness.

But what does "team effectiveness" mean? In this book, team effectiveness is seen as having three main components:

1. Task effectiveness is the extent to which the team is successful in achieving its task-related objectives.

2. Mental health refers to the well-being, growth and development of team members.

3. Team viability is the probability that a team will continue to work together and function effectively.

While the above elements are necessary for any team to be effective, and while the processes that teams go through are the same, there are several characteristics that are unique to the top team which impact upon the functioning of the top management group.

DISTINCTIVE CHARACTERISTICS OF A TOP TEAM

Prominence of the external environment

While many groups need to interact beyond the boundaries of their group, the TMG has a very unique relationship with the external environment in that it fulfils both boundary spanning and information scanning roles. TMGs and the environment they operate in have a reciprocal relationship. Several elements have a major impact on the group, for example competitors, shareholders, markets and customers. One of the central and most complex tasks the TMG has to deal with is understanding and managing this environment.

The task

One of the top team's most difficult tasks is to predict and manage an ever-changing environmental context, increasingly characterised by hyper-competitive forces. Because of the strategic nature of the TMG's business, the tasks involved are often extremely complex with multiple components. They both formulate and implement adaptive responses to the environment. This requires crafting a delicate balance between creative conflict, in order to formulate a response, and group consensus, to implement the decision. Such a finely tuned balancing act can often fail.

In its "market intelligence" role, the top group regularly experiences information overload and ambiguity, as it receives multiple signals or stimuli from the external environment.[7] These signals can be open to perceptual bias, political manipulation and many differing interpretations which will ultimately have an impact upon the organisation. The strategic significance of the decision-making process and the implementation of such decisions is what differentiates such teams from lower level groups. Top groups may, therefore, be characterised as complex decision-making groups.

No bounded time frame

Except in extreme cases (new organisations or new management groups) top management groups experience no clear beginning or end to their work and the functioning of such teams is best examined longitudinally. Further, the team may face abstract goals such as "improve company performance" or "implement the company's strategy" which can prove too broad to provide the appropriate focus or any clear time frame that is necessary for coordinated, directed effort.[8]

The management of polarities

The top team is often faced with the task of balancing what may, at first, appear to be mutually exclusive goals. The management of the tension between short term vs. long term, task vs. people, management vs. leadership, individual heads of functions vs. top team membership, stability vs. change and competition vs. cooperation requires a tolerance of ambiguity and a comfort with change and paradox.

Locus of top management groups

Because members of this group occupy the upper ranks of the organisation, their actions will carry great symbolic significance. The members of the group themselves will frequently head up their own sub-organisations/functions. This can create a conflict regarding group identity – do members see themselves as leaders of their sub-organisation or members of the top group? This conflict raises important questions about the validity of the top team metaphor.

The composition of the top group

The individuals comprising the top group tend to be people who have displayed significant accomplishments throughout their career; they tend to be achievement oriented and, as a consequence, would expect and require a considerable degree of autonomy and decision-making discretion.[9] Close supervision may not be welcomed and team members undertake many initiatives on their own. This tendency to work in a solitary manner also raises questions about the validity of the team definition. Group composition can also lead to intensified political behaviour – members tend to be ambitious and the ultimate goal for many top group members is succession to the position of CEO. This "succession tournament" can lead to politics and competitive behaviour being more pronounced within such groups. In the run up to the final selection of the CEO, particularly in organisations where trust levels are low, each member of the group may attempt to portray the others in a negative light, leading to organisational atrophy which can extend to as long as two years.

CONCEPTUAL ELEMENTS OF A TOP TEAM

The workings of the TMG are multifaceted. Hambrick has outlined some of these components, which include the composition, structure, processes and leadership of the group.[10] To gain a complete understanding of the functioning of the top group, it is important to consider the interaction of these variables operating as a dynamic cluster.

Composition

The collective characteristics of the top management group members have been documented as having a very significant effect on the outcome of the organisation. Research has focused on the demographic composition of top group members including the job tenure, age, functional speciality, personality and educational background.[11] The effects of such characteristics on the effectiveness of the TMG have been shown to be pervasive, with studies linking heterogeneity of top groups to such outcomes as performance, management turnover and consensus. This will be discussed in the next chapter.

It is important to note here that a special area of interest is not only the quantity of a compositional characteristic but also the dispersion of that characteristic. For example, not only is the average tenure of group members of interest to researchers but also the level of diversity of tenures as predictors of social integration or diversity of perspective. To take a simple example, new

Figure 1.2: The Conceptual Elements of the Top Management Group

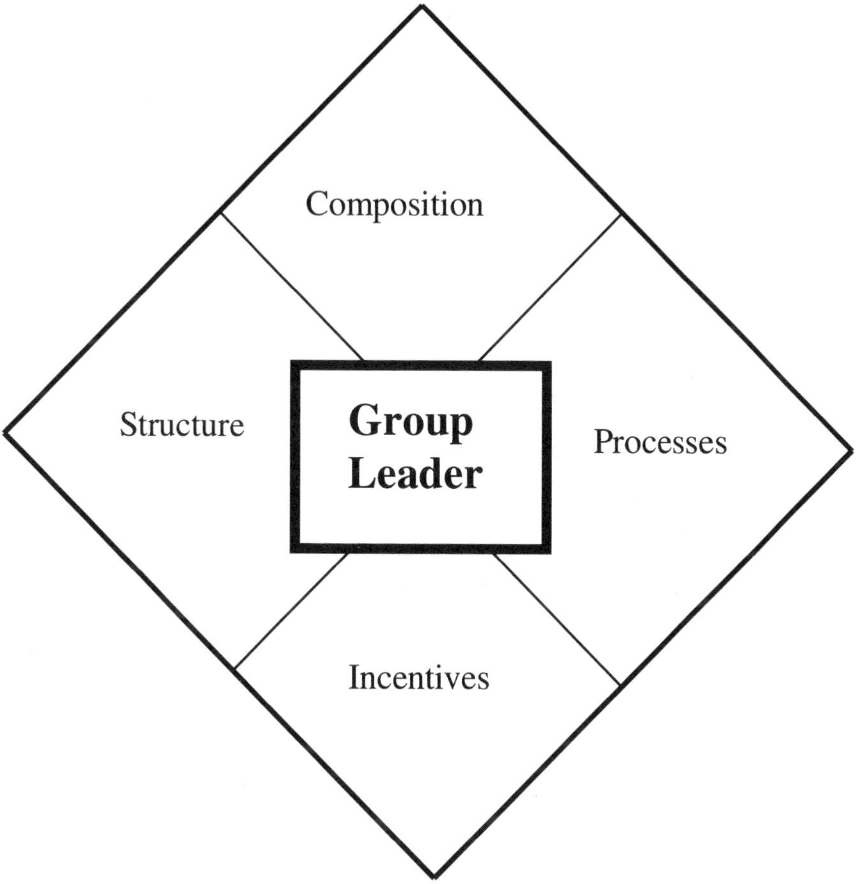

Composition

Structure

**Group
Leader**

Processes

Incentives

Adapted from Hambrick, D. 1994. Top Management Groups: A Conceptual Integration and Reconsideration of the Label "Team". *Research in Organisational Behaviour*, 16:171-213.

individuals joining the team at the same time are likely to undergo a shared socialisation experience which is different to that of existing team members. Existing team members in turn may have developed shared norms and routines which may conflict with the "new blood" recruits. A benefit of newcomers is that they do not possess the burden of history which long tenure top members suffer. To use a phrase in vogue "goldfish don't see the water they swim in!" The importance of TMG composition and the consequent effects on organisational strategy and performance will be discussed in a later chapter.

Structure

This refers to the roles of members and the relationships among those roles, the central element being the degree of task independence of members. In any team there is bound to be a degree of role ambiguity and overlap. However, due to the often heterogeneous composition of the top group, role ambiguity is often accentuated. Members tend to be ambitious and by the time they have reached top management many have adopted an executive leadership discipline that is grounded in the principle of individual accountability. Top level executives are often uncomfortable collaborating in "amorphous groups with overlapping accountabilities".[12] Such an overlap of accountabilities would occur when there is a conflict between the TMG members' roles as functional or departmental leaders and their roles as members of the top management group.

A frequent dilemma facing top groups is whether members see their role as being head of their function or an equal member of a group. One of the root causes of some problems of TMG's is that members have indistinct or conflicting views about the role of the group and what their own role within the group is. There is a need to clarify what is expected from each member of the group, both in terms of generic expectations (the general team behaviour expected) as well as the more specific expectations of individual TMG members, based on position, role in organisation and role in team.[13] TMG size is also an important aspect of structure. The size of a TMG varies. In a study of US high technology companies based in Ireland, we found that the size ranges from two to eleven members, with an average of between five and six.

Incentives

What are the inducements, both explicit and implicit, that are presented to TMGs? Surprisingly, this has received little attention. A particularly salient inducement for top group members is the prospect of rising to the highest position of team leader or CEO. The "succession tournament" has been seen as one of the major incentives propelling the behaviour of top executives. Top group members, in general, tend to be ambitious, achievement and power-oriented individuals who are very much affected by succession prospects.[14] Vancil observed that the succession tournament varied according to factors such as age and tenure of the CEO in office, corporate performance and the number of eligible contenders. The extent to which incentives are tied to the overall collective performance of the group, to individual performance or to other factors is a very powerful determinant of group behaviour. Research on lower level groups has found that collective incentives tied to performance of the group, not surprisingly, tended to lead to more collaborative behaviour. However, in our research on TMGs in US multinationals based in Ireland, 98 per cent of respondents felt their salary was in no way affected by the performance of the TMG as a whole, and 71 per cent responded that group cash bonuses were not applicable. It appears that TMGs' incentives are still based individually rather than collectively. However, there is a dearth of research conducted in the area of top team incentives.

Processes

The third major element of a TMG is its processes. Processes can be defined as "the nature of interaction among top managers as they engage in strategic decision making".[15] Communication flows, sociopolitical dynamics, group decision dynamics, group decision processes, coalition formation, conflict resolution and social integration are all dimensions of team process. Team functioning and team reflexivity can be enhanced by considering the principal aspects of teamwork:

- team objectives

- participation in teams

- task orientation

- support for innovation.

What makes TMG processes different from other groups is the level of politicisation[16] and power distribution[17] within top managerial groups that may not be present elsewhere.

Group leader

Although it is becoming more accepted that management is a shared effort, the CEO is still the most influential member. Research has documented that despite the fact that it is the TMG rather than the CEO which is the best predictor of organisational outcomes,[18] it is the CEO who is crucial in shaping and making this top group work. Indeed, it is the CEO who so often selects this top group. In our study of TMGs in US multinationals, 44 per cent of respondents felt it was true to say the CEO made the final decision of hiring a TMG member alone and a further 22 per cent felt this statement was definitely true. Recent research has shown that the characteristics of the CEO (for example personality, cognitive style and values) are related to the strategies pursued by the company and also overall performance. The characteristics and leadership style of the CEO will be discussed in a later chapter.

Ultimately, all the core elements of the TMG influence each other. Composition of the group will influence processes; structure will affect incentives; group leadership will affect structure.

HOW THE CONTEXT SHAPES THE TMG

The TMG does not exist in isolation, nor does the organisation itself. A mutual relationship exists between the organisation and its context. The context consists of both external and internal factors, all of which need to be analysed in order to achieve team effectiveness.

Cultural and societal norms need to be looked at. For example, today's customers and employees are more highly educated and sophisticated than their predecessors. Top management need to be trained to deal effectively in this new climate. Also cultural differences need to be fully understood when managing cross national management teams, increasingly common in the modern distributed e-business environment.

What is the business environment? What are the strengths, weaknesses, opportunities and threats posed by the external business context? How turbulent is the business environment? Environmental stability affects the composition of the TMG.[19] Environmental instability has been found to lead to lower ages, reduced tenure and demographic heterogeneity of the group. Therefore, a key question to ask is how old is the industry? For example, the age of an industry can have a very significant effect on the basic composition of the top group, in terms of members' ages, tenure, education and homogeneity.[20]

What is the mission of the corporation? What is the corporation's role? What are the growth projections and the firm's technology capabilities? What are the firm's social, political and commercial values? Is there a policy of strict cost control? Obviously, a mandate for growth will require a different management style to that of cost control. It can also affect the power distribution within the TMG. Hambrick found that in organisations where the mandate was one of cost control, members whose expertise and knowledge were efficiency oriented (for example accounting) held disproportionate influence within the TMG.[21] Miles and Snow found that prospector firms (firms that compete using product innovation) have relatively higher representation of marketing and product development experts within their TMGs than defender organisations who compete on the basis of a stable product line.[22]

Another influence is organisational performance. Organisational performance will affect the amount of stability within the TMG. The more satisfactory the performance, the more stable the group. In extreme cases, this can lead to complacency and a lack of innovation within the group.[23] On the other hand, conditions of poor organisational performance can lead to a state of extreme stress, with closed information channels and perceptual distortions.[24]

HOW THE TMG SHAPES THE CONTEXT

Not only does the context affect the composition and behaviour of the top management group but vice versa. It is probably safe to say that within most

oganisations, no other small group has as great a potential to influence the
fate of the enterprise as the top group. Many studies have documented how
the composition of the top group (age, tenure, diversity of the members) affects the strategy and performance of the organisation, many with conflicting
results. Indeed, there is a mutual relationship between the TMG and the strategy and performance of the enterprise, with all elements influencing each
other. TMGs simultaneously shape and are shaped by their surroundings.

Studies have been conducted exploring the effects of TMGs on different
elements of organisation strategy (see Table 1.1). Hambrick argues that too
little attention has been given to the mechanisms that serve to convert group
characteristics into group outcomes. In his view, investigations of top groups
should connect group composition, processes, structures and incentives in
order to achieve a complete understanding of the effects of TMGs on strategy
and performance.

Table 1.1: Elements of Organisational Strategy[25]

Strategic risk	Degree to which the firm's strategy is exposed to external threats, such as a strong material supplier (e.g. a single supplier of a critical resource); a dominant customer; and powerful capital suppliers.
Strategic innovation	Development of new products and services and the creative penetration of new markets as part of the company's strategy.
Strategic differentiation	Does the firm invest in building a perception of uniqueness or quality in the mind of the customer?

While composition and diversity of the top group and the subsequent organisation effects will be discussed in detail in Chapter 2, it is worth noting here
the contradictory nature of much of the research. For example, tenure similarity has been positively related in some studies to frequency of communication, social integration and strategic innovation.[26] However, in contrast to this
finding is Ancona and Caldwell's research which found that tenure diversity
had a positive effect on internal group dynamics, which were related to high
team performance.[27]

A management study by the Maryland Business School Faculty has found
that the greater the social integration and sharing of power between top management groups, the greater the risk in the company's strategy.[28] It is important to differentiate here between intentional and unintentional risk. While
intentional risk can be desirable in that it can result in better organisation
performance, unintentional risk is the result of poor decision making and can
be detrimental. Interestingly, no relationship was found to exist between TMG

background diversity and strategic risk. Another very interesting result of this study was that while strategic innovation was positively related to social integration, there was no relationship found between strategic innovation and TMG diversity. They also found that TMG diversity (age, experience, education, tenure) was negatively related to organisation performance, defined in terms of profitability and returns on assets and investments. Such findings contradict much research on diversity and innovation which would indicate that diversity is necessary for innovation. However, this is because of the complexity of the effects of diversity on teams. The results differ depending on whether the diversity is task-related or relations-oriented. Task-related diversity includes physical skills and abilities as well as cognitive knowledge, skills, abilities and job experience, whereas relations-oriented diversity includes social status, attitudes, values and personality.[29] With diversity come multiple perspectives which can often lead to conflict. Such conflict can undermine any benefits that diversity may bring, however, this is dependent on the type of conflict which occurs. Schweiger et al state that "on the one hand, conflict improves decision quality; on the other, it may weaken the ability of the group to work together".[30] It is the effects of interconnected processes such as conflict, consensus and trust within the team that will ultimately determine whether diversity is an advantage or a hindrance.

It is also important to note that much of the research on diversity in teams has been conducted on lower level teams. While many of the team processes remain the same no matter what level the team is, there are certain factors that will influence results. Top groups are composed of individuals who tend to be ambitious and individualistic and there are few group incentives of a financial nature at the top. These factors may mean that findings related to diversity may differ, depending on whether we are studying TMGs or groups at lower levels in the corporation.

Researchers such as Janis have investigated whether the internal processes of the policy group are the central determinant of policy quality or organisation performance. Eisenhardt and Bourgeois concluded that politics, "the observable, but often covert, actions by which executives enhance their power", can lead to intergroup competitiveness, leading to restricted flow of information and thus have a negative impact on organisation performance.[31] Politics in the top management group will be addressed in a later chapter. These studies suggest that the TMG composition does significantly influence the fate of the organisation. Top groups, through their interpretation of their surroundings and their choice of strategy, "enact a certain environment".[32]

CONCLUSION

In this chapter, we set out to highlight the importance of studying the top management group. We discuss the problem of terminology when describing the collection of top executives in the organisation. We state our position in this dilemma – we use the term top management group to describe those occupying the "upper echelons". We recognise that not all members of the upper echelons display many of the attributes of "teamness", i.e. inter-dependence, cohesion, high levels of communication, mutual accountability and so on. However, we believe that the goal of achieving effective top teams can be accomplished and is a goal worth striving for.

In the following chapters, we explore the deterrents to TMGs transform-ing to TMTs and how to overcome them. As a result, while we use the term top team throughout the remainder of the book, we are of course actively aware of the top management group versus top management team distinction. We now turn to the critical issue of selecting the top management team.

Chapter 2

Selection of the Top Team

INTRODUCTION

Building teamwork at the top poses a number of questions for those in the position of designing and shaping a top management team. Organisations frequently fail to have appropriate mechanisms in place to encourage true team spirit among their top managers. In the previous chapter, we discussed some of the reasons that prevent top managers becoming top teams – members are ambitious and individualistic, and are less prepared to participate effectively within a team than their colleagues at lower levels.[1] They usually juggle two very different roles, that of functional head and corporate team member, roles that often come into conflict. Also, the top team task is particularly complex and ambiguous, and our own research indicates that few group incentive schemes exist at the top. Such deterrents should not go unexamined when selecting and building a top team. They need to be confronted openly and managed in an appropriate manner.

SELECTING YOUR TEAM – IDENTIFYING THE IDEAL TEAM PROFILE

Establishing the ideal team profile can be done in two ways. It may be done in broad overall terms or, alternatively, on a position by position basis. The latter is the preferred option as there may be certain characteristics desired in all members and yet others which are desirable only in certain positions.[2]

Hambrick proposes that a suitable approach for profiling the top team would be to outline very broad areas of managerial qualities and leave the specific dimensions to the CEO of the organisation. The choice of specific qualities should be based on precise analysis of the internal and external environment, as well as on what the CEO feels would be a suitable fit. Hambrick outlines some of the broad areas that should be addressed by the CEO which we will briefly discuss below.

Values

Hambrick maintains that this is the first criterion that needs to be considered when profiling a top team. Finkelstein and Hambrick define values as "a broad and relatively enduring preference for some state of affairs".[3] While there are many value dimensions, Hambrick and Brandon[4] attempted a consolidation of five important value schemes, resulting in the six value dimensions below:

Collectivism: to value the wholeness of humankind and of social systems; regard and respect for all people

Duty: to value the integrity of reciprocal relationships; obligation and loyalty

Rationality: to value fact-based, emotion-free decisions and actions

Novelty: to value change, the new and the different

Materialism: to value wealth and tangible possessions

Power: to value control of situations and people

Values affect the team members' contributions in three ways:

1. Values cause executives to prefer certain behaviours and outcomes to others.

2. Values affect the scanning and filtering out of data used in decision making – people tend to filter information that is inconsistent with their existing values and attitudes. Values also affect selective perception in interpretation. For example, a manager who values rationality would be uncomfortable with ambiguous tasks, preferring to digest quantitative, incremental data. Our experience with top teams indicates that rationality is an important value within top teams.

3. Values affect the person's receptivity to any incentives and norms the general manager may try to establish. Some members may value status and recognition while others may value self-actualisation and achievement. An effective CEO should engage in continual observation of team members and develop an awareness of their different values and hence, incentives that will motivate them. For example, an individual who values collectivism will be motivated by very different incentives than an individual who values materialism.

Another typology establishing a link between values and incentives is that of Cohen and Bradford.[5] They identify five different value currencies: inspiration related currencies (for example vision, ethics), task related currencies (for example new resources), position related currencies (for example recognition, reputation), relationship related currencies (for example belongingness, support) and personal related currencies (for example self-concept, autonomy, self-actualisation). The currency an individual values will dictate the incentive that will inspire them to excellence.

Aptitudes

Positions on the team also need to be mapped out according to what aptitudes are required among members. Hambrick defined aptitudes "as personal capabilities not amenable to short term change" and cited creativity, intellect, tolerance for ambiguity and interpersonal skills as examples.[6] Again, depending on the organisation, different aptitudes will be required for different situations. For example, using Miles and Snow's model, in a company that competes using product innovation (prospectors), where the environment is in flux and turbulent, aptitudes such as tolerance for ambiguity and creativity would be prerequisites. In a company competing in a stable environment (defenders), essential aptitudes would be of a more analytical nature.

Skills

A certain mix of skills is also required, something Katzenbach has found absent in many top teams.[7] Skills are more concrete than values and aptitudes, and are more amenable to change. Top team members can be trained to improve skills such as communication, presentation, negotiation, interpersonal skills, planning skills and delegation.

Knowledge

Certain in-depth knowledge will be required within the team. For example, expertise may be needed in certain industries, technical or functional area issues, legal or regulatory factors, or market place trends to name but a few. The more technically complex the organisation, the more knowledge required. According to Hambrick, this area is the most responsive to immediate change and this can be achieved through education and training.

Cognitive style

Individuals differ considerably in how they process information and make decisions. While the difference is not so straight forward as right brain and left brain thinking, there have been major distinctions widely accepted among psychologists. Jung maintains that we become aware of ideas, facts and occurrences (how we perceive things) using either sensing (a conscious process) or intuition (a subconscious process). When using sensing, perception occurs literally through the use of the five senses. As a result, this type is very much rooted in the present, practical, orderly and dislikes ambiguity.[8]

Intuition (discerning patterns, gaps or relationships among stimuli), alternatively, is a subconscious process, rather than a conscious sensory experience. Ideas appear to "come out of the blue". They are future oriented, always looking ahead and inspiring others with innovations. While those with a preference for sensing focus on the details, the intuitor concentrates on the big picture.

Jung also maintained that there are two ways of making judgements about one's perceptions, namely by thinking or by feeling.[9] Thinking is a logical and analytical process based on objectives and principles, whereas feeling is a personal, subjective process, based on the individual's values. The mix of thinkers and feelers/sensers and intuitors will greatly affect the team's strategic decisions – both at the formulation and implementation stages. Our research indicates that the preferred way of making judgements for senior managers is that of thinking. In order to get to a senior position, one must make tough decisions, be self-critical and objective. This is very much reflected in the top teams that we have come into contact with. However, many of these teams are aware that the qualities required to reach a top position may be quite different to the qualities required to remain there and many TMTs are realising the necessity to tap into the more feeling oriented behaviours which are linked with emotional intelligence, a subject we return to in our chapter on leadership.

The context in which the team works will also greatly determine the appropriate mix. For example, when working within an ever-changing, highly technological and competitive environment (a prospector organisation), a highly analytical team with no intuitors would be unsuitable. Such a team would be more suited to a defender type industry.

Disposition

The "intangible aura, style, or demeanor" of members is the final area that Hambrick draws attention to. This refers to qualities such as enthusiasm, warmth and poise that are present within the management team. As the top team carries more symbolic significance than lower level teams, TMTs need to provide an outward measure of legitimacy. The qualities required vary with the industry and the structure of the organisation. A hierarchical, status based organisation, such as that traditionally found in banking and the civil service, may require members of the TMT to remain distant, a friendly phantom. However, in a flatter, more organic organisation, such as that characterised in the software development industry, high social distance may be considered inappropriate.

WHO SELECTS THE TOP MANAGEMENT TEAM?

The CEO of an ongoing business is rarely in the position of selecting an entire top team. Usually, many members of the top management team are already in place and this is often a reflection of the members' formal position within the hierarchy. It is only partly true to say that the CEO is the sole shaper of the team and often the main selector of new team members. Our research indicates that, in many organisations, the membership of the TMT is often a *fait accomplis* unless the new CEO actually decides to restructure the team. However, that is not to say that the gap between the ideal TMT and the actual TMT cannot and should not be narrowed. Indeed, it is this creative tension between the actual and the potential that often spurs a TMT to new heights. However, in order to do this, the existing team needs to be assessed.

We have already outlined some of the areas that need to be addressed when selecting a top team. Such factors also hold relevance when assessing the team. The correct fit will depend on many factors including the industry itself, the organisational goals, values and performance and the external environment amongst others. The managerial qualities that would be desirable in a defender company's TMT would be very different to those required in a prospector company's TMT. An effective CEO should diagnose the most appropriate "fit" depending on what type of organisation is being dealt with, the external/internal environment and the business needs (see Figure 2.1).

Figure 2.1: Top Management Team Formation

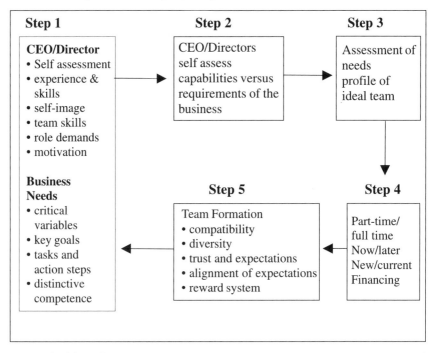

Source: Smith, K.G., Presentation to Conference: Teamwork at the Top, College of Business, University of Limerick, May, 1994

TEAM ROLES, PERSONALITY AND TEAM PERFORMANCE

As we have already discussed, the abilities, values and behaviours of TMT members are crucial to the performance of teams. Relevant to this are the roles that team members play. Roles, "the patterns of behaviour expected by others from a person occupying a certain position in an organisational hierarchy"[10] can be thought of in two ways. The first is in terms of functional roles. Such roles are often the basis of membership within the team, these being considered most appropriate to the task(s) which the team has to perform.[11] While the correct functional fit is necessary in terms of experience and expertise for the task in hand, this will not necessarily help when it comes to how a TMT makes and implements strategic decisions. Functional roles offer no direction on how members approach problems, interact with one another and their style of behaviour in general. The second is in terms of what Belbin refers to as team roles, the different mix of personalities in the team and their tendency to behave in distinctive ways.

Personality and teamwork at the top

Experience of working in teams suggests that personalities play an important part in the effectiveness of teams working together. The questions often raised are:

"What types of people work best together?"
"What sort of mix of personalities is needed for a team to be effective?"
"In what ways must group members be compatible in order to work together effectively?"

A number of models of personality in teams have been proposed in the psychological literature. For example, many organisations have tried to achieve compatibility within teams in the cognitive styles of members, by using the Myers-Briggs Type Indicator (MBTI) assessment instrument (a Jungian based questionnaire measure of cognitive style). The MBTI provides a useful measure of personality preferences that all people use at different times. These eight preferences are then organised into four bi-polar scales (see Figure 2.2). Your type is determined by the four preferences that you "voted for" when answering the questions on the MBTI.

Figure 2.2: The Four Scales Measured by the MBTI

Scale	Refers to	Key Activity
Extraversion-Introversion	How a person is energised	Energising
Sensing-Intuition	What a person pays attention to	Attending
Thinking-Feeling	How a person decides	Deciding
Judging-Perceiving	What lifestyle a person adopts	Living

However, there is little research evidence presently available showing a relationship between compatibility and team performance.

Another popular approach is Belbin's Team Roles Model.[12] Through the use of Belbin's self perception inventory, one is able to obtain an indication of one's team role types. Belbin defined the "team role" as the "tendency to behave, contribute and interrelate with others at work in certain distinctive ways". It is important to emphasise that Belbin discriminated sharply between a person's "team role" and their "functional role". "Functional role" refers to the person supplying the requisite technical skills and operational knowledge required by the team. People appointed to a certain job are, therefore, likely to vary greatly in their "team role", while their "functional role" may be very similar.

It is also important to distinguish between an individual's team role and their personality, "the psychological qualities that influence an individual's characteristic behaviour patterns in a broadly distinctive and consistent manner, across different situations and through time".[13] Team roles and personality should not be used interchangeably. Belbin views personality as an independent predictor of team role behaviour. He argues that there are nine team role types (Table 2.1) which people display and that it is important to achieve a balance of these within a team. His view is that a mix of the nine team role types is required for a team to perform effectively. Individuals themselves will usually have a mix of team role types in their personality profiles. Within teams of only three or four individuals there may, nevertheless, be primary and secondary team role types which cover the nine areas of team role functioning. Thus, as well as contributing their professional skills to the team, members also contribute particular behavioural characteristics which can be identified with natural team roles. Team role theory demonstrates that for a team to be high performing, it is necessary to achieve a balance of both functional roles and team roles.

Table 2.1: Belbin's Nine Team Roles

Belbin's team role theory
Based on research with over 200 teams conducting management business games at the Administrative Staff College, Henley, in the UK, Belbin identified nine team types. Almost always, people have a mix of roles and will have dominant and sub-dominant roles.

Coordinator
The coordinator is a person-oriented leader. This person is trusting, accepting, dominant and is committed to team goals and objectives. The coordinator is a positive thinker who approves of goal attainment, struggle and effort in others. The coordinator is "someone tolerant enough always

to listen to others, but strong enough to reject their advice". The coordinator may not stand out in a team and usually does not have a sharp intellect.

Shaper
The shaper is a task-focussed leader, who abounds in nervous energy, who has high motivation to achieve and for whom winning is the name of the game. The shaper is committed to achieving ends and will "shape" others into achieving the aims of the team. Shapers will challenge, argue or disagree and will display aggression in the pursuit of goal achievement. Two or three shapers in a group, according to Belbin, can lead to conflict, aggravation and in-fighting.

Plant
The plant is a specialist idea maker characterized by high IQ and introversion, while also being dominant and original. The plant tends to take radical approaches to team functioning and problems. Plants are more concerned with major issues than with details. Weaknesses are a tendency to disregard practical details and argumentativeness.

Resource investigator
"The resource investigator is the executive who is never in his room, and if he is, he is on the telephone." The resource investigator is someone who explores opportunities and develops contacts. Resource investigators are good negotiators who probe others for information and support and pick up other people's ideas and develop them. They are characterized by sociability and enthusiasm and are good at liaison work and exploring resources outside the group. Weaknesses are a tendency to lose interest after initial fascination with an idea, and they are not usually a source of original ideas.

Company worker/implementer
The implementer is aware of external obligations and is disciplined, conscientious and has a good self-image. Implementers tend to be tough-minded and practical, trusting and tolerant, respecting established traditions. They are characterized by low anxiety and tend to work for the team in a practical, realistic way. Implementers figure prominently in positions of responsibility in larger organisations. They tend to do the jobs that others do not want to do and do them well (for example, disciplining employees). Implementers are conservative, inflexible and slow to respond to new possibilities.

Monitor evaluator
According to the model, this is a judicious, prudent, intelligent person with a low need to achieve. Monitor evaluators contribute particularly at times

of crucial decision making because they are capable of evaluating competing proposals. The monitor evaluator is not deflected by emotional arguments, is serious-minded, tends to be slow in coming to a decision because of a need to think things over and takes pride in never being wrong. Weaknesses are that they may appear dry and boring or even over-critical. They are not good at inspiring others. Those in high level appointments are often monitor evaluators.

Team worker
The team worker makes helpful interventions to avert potential friction and enables difficult characters within the team to use their skills to positive ends. Team workers tend to keep team spirit up and allow other members to contribute effectively. Their diplomatic skills together with their sense of humour are assets to a team. They tend to have skills in listening, coping with awkward people and to be sociable, sensitive and people-oriented. They tend to be indecisive in moments of crisis and reluctant to do things that might hurt others.

Completer finisher
The completer finisher dots the i's and crosses the t's. Complete finishers give attention to detail, aim to complete and to do so thoroughly. They make steady effort and are consistent in their work. They are not so interested in the glamour of spectacular success. Weaknesses, according to Belbin, are that they tend to be over anxious and have difficulty letting go and delegating work.

Specialist
The specialist provides knowledge and technical skills which are in rare supply within the team. Specialists are often highly introverted and anxious, and tend to be self-starting, dedicated and committed. Their weaknesses are single-mindedness and a lack of interest in other peoples' subjects.

Team roles and a team's key stage of activity

Belbin also stresses the link between the stages of a team's project or activities and the need for different team roles to be dominant at different stages. Table 2.2 lists the six stages with Belbin's comments on the team roles deemed relevant to each stage.

Belbin claimed to be able to predict team performance through knowledge of each team members team role ("balanced" teams were predicted to be high performers).

However, in Belbin's original work, team performance was measured in terms of winning and losing. Difficulties occur when there are no objective measures with which to judge team performance, as is the case for management teams or, in Katzenbach and Smith's terms, teams classified as "recommending things" or "running things" rather than those which "make or do things".[14] In TMTs where little if any objective criteria exist to measure performance of the team, some form of subjective criteria has to be established. Research has shown little agreement on what that criteria should be. Barbara Senior, in testing the validity of Belbin's role theory for TMTs, asked each team to set its own team criteria and rate its performance accordingly.[15] This process is recommended by theorists such as Galpin who says "asking teams and individuals to rate themselves on whatever factors are determined to be important is a good way to approach 'immeasurables' like customer care, team work and communication skills".[16] Senior, using this process, established a link between "balanced" TMTs and high performance.

Table 2.2: Team Roles Relevant to Different Stages of a Team's Project

Key stages of team activity	Team roles relevant to particular stages
1. Identifying needs	Key figures at this stage are individuals with a strong goal awareness. Shapers and coordinators make their mark here.
2. Finding ideas	Once an objective is set, the means of achieving it are required. Here plants and resource investigators have a crucial role to play.
3. Formulating plans	Two activities help ideas turn into plans. One weighing up the options, another making good use of all relevant experience and knowledge to ensure a good decision. Monitor evaluators make especially good long-term planners and specialists have a key role to play at this stage.
4. Making contacts	People must be persuaded that an improvement is possible. Champions of the plans and cheerleaders must be found. This is an activity where resource investigators are in their element. However, to appease disturbed groups, a team worker is required.
5. Establishing the organisation	Plans need turning into procedures, methods and working practices to become routines. Imple-

	menters are the people required here. These routines, however, need people to make them work. Getting people to fit the system is what coordinators are good at.
6. Following through	Too many assumptions are made that all will work out well in the end. Good follow-through benefits from the attentions of completers. Implementers, too, pull their weight in this area, for they pride themselves on being efficient in anything they undertake.

Adapted from Senior, B. 1997. Team Roles and Team Performance: Is There "Really" a Link? *Journal of Occupational and Organisational Psychology*, 70(3): 241-259.

However, it is important to note that establishment of an individual's team role does not necessarily predict behaviour. Earlier in the chapter, we discussed the importance of values, cognitive abilities and disposition of the TMT. Belbin, too, found personality, mental ability, values and motivations to play a significant part in predicting behaviour.

Belbin referred to these predictors as overriders (see Figure 2.3 overleaf) and maintained that personality, mental ability and experience (a "momentous event in business life which has a lasting effect in changing someone's approach") could override an individual's chosen role type in predicting behaviour.

Field constraints (context) play a significant part in determining team role behaviour, according to Belbin. This is when people inhibit their natural behaviour or change its form to take account of immediate factors in the environment, for example if a boss is present, times of stress and so on.

The final overriding factor identified by Belbin is what he terms "role learning" where individuals participate in education on team skills. By recognising the roles of others and by becoming aware of the range of roles that are available to the self, along with those that are not, people learn to modify their behaviour to take account of the situation. Therefore, it becomes possible to manage an association with others for whom an individual feels no natural affinity.

Factors that may override team role behaviour

Belbin maintained that team role behaviour could be outweighed under certain circumstances. For example, psycho-physiological factors, especially extraversion-introversion and high anxiety-low anxiety, can underlie behaviour. Belbin also found high level mental ability could override personality to generate exceptional behaviour. Belbin's third overrider was values and he

Figure 2.3: Belbin's "Overriders"

Belbin's model outlining factors that determine role behaviour:

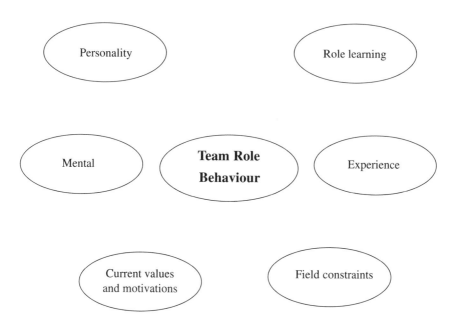

maintained that certain firmly held values could lead to a certain type of behaviour. One of Belbin's overriders that has received much attention is that of the immediate environment. Shi and Tang maintain that it is the nature of the organisational task environment that sets the field constraints for organisational members, influences their values and motivations, frames their experience and defines their role learning.[17] Other overriders mentioned by Belbin as strongly affecting behaviour in teams are personal experience and cultural factors.

Top team diversity and the consequences for team performance

Is heterogeneity advantageous or disadvantageous to the effective functioning of the top team? Is diversity in personality, cognitive style, background, age, tenure, education within TMTs a good thing? Or are TMTs and their members impeded by such differences? There is no simple answer to the above questions. Much of the research available on diversity within top teams offers contradictory results, indicating that diversity can have both positive and negative outcomes depending on how team processes are managed within the team. For diversity to lead to innovation and quality decisions, processes such as conflict need to be processed in the interests of effective decision making and task performance rather than on the basis of egotistical motivation to win or prevail. This in turn will generate improved performance and more innovative action will be the result. However, this is a lot easier in theory than it is in practice.

Figure 2.4: The Effects of Top Team Heterogeneity on TMT Performance

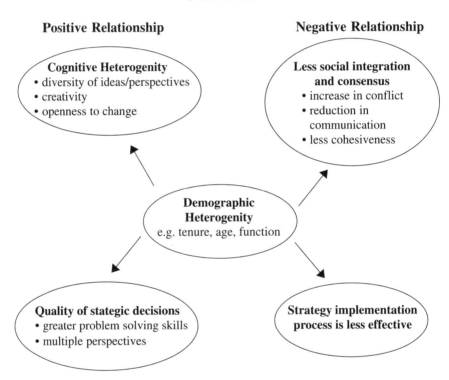

Adapted from Finkelstein, S. and Hambrick, D. 1996. *Strategic Leadership: Top Executives and their Effects on Organisations.* West Publishing Company.

One prevalent notion is that if teams are composed of people with different backgrounds, personalities, skills and experiences, they will bring different perspectives to the group decision-making process. Demographic heterogeneity may be seen as a proxy for cognitive heterogeneity representing innovativeness, problem solving abilities and diversity of information sources and perspectives.[18]

Research indicates that such diversity will lead to more alternatives in strategic decision making, a more stringent evaluation of those alternatives and, therefore, higher quality decisions. Thus, it may be concluded that cognitive diversity may be positively associated with the quality of strategic decision making.

However, while team diversity is seen to have a positive effect on the *quality* of decisions, this may hold no organisational benefits if such decisions fail to be implemented. In order to understand the relationship between top team composition and organisational outcomes, the effects of heterogeneity on processes such as consensual decision making and conflict must be investigated. Of course, other organisational processes such as power also intermediate in the strategic decision-making process. Finkelstein suggests that a "recognition of the role of power in strategic choice and a means of incorporating power" into research on team diversity and the organisational effects is necessary in order to obtain a more complete picture.[19] Because CEOs are generally more influential than other members, this disparity in power should also be taken into consideration in assessing the management of conflict within the top management group. Conflict and power in the top team will be further explored in later chapters.

It would appear that while there is a positive relationship between group heterogeneity and the quality of strategic decisions, there is a negative relationship between heterogeneity and the implementation of such decisions. It is the relationship between TMT heterogeneity and group processes (social integration, interpersonal conflict and strategic decision making) that potentially affects organisational outcomes such as strategic choice.

One reason offered by Amason to explain these paradoxical effects is the domino effect heterogeneity has on team conflict.[20] He has identified two types of conflict: cognitive/task conflict which is task oriented and focuses on judgemental differences as to how to achieve the best solution; and affective/relationship conflict which is focused on personal incompatibilities and interpersonal disputes.

Research has shown that the different types of conflict have very different consequences for the satisfaction levels and performance of the team.[21] Like the issue of heterogeneity, the positive aspects and the negative aspects are very closely intertwined. Heterogeneity in team composition has been found to increase cognitive conflict, but also to increase the instances of affective conflict. While cognitive conflict has been shown to enhance the quality of strategic decision making, affective conflict can erode these benefits. The emergence of affective conflict and the devastating effects it can have on decision implementation highlights the dilemma facing senior team members; how to tap into the positive outcomes of team heterogeneity while curbing the negative outcomes. This means harnessing the effects of cognitive conflict while preventing this conflict from deteriorating into affective conflict. The problems associated with this balancing act will be discussed in more depth in Chapter 5.

CONCLUSION

In this chapter, we have discussed the importance of the top team profile. We have discussed the importance of values, aptitudes, skills, knowledge and disposition when selecting or assessing your top team. The importance of a "balanced team" regarding both functional and team roles was illustrated. The necessity to include group structure and processes when discussing team diversity was also highlighted – to omit processes such as interpersonal conflict and consensual decision making would result in research that is misleading and potentially dangerous for executives. Such processes can often erode the benefits of a heterogeneous team. For example, interpersonal conflict can prevent rich, innovative strategic decisions from being implemented. Highly competitive organisations require a heterogeneous group of senior managers with differing perceptions of the world, yet with the ability to participate in the process that surmounts these different views to enact a complex organisational reality.[22] While such top teams may be difficult to achieve, there are many that have the potential to reach these goals. It is one of the purposes of this book to draw attention to this potential and very real danger and to provide ways of overcoming the obstacles that group processes can present when striving for creativity, innovation and high performance.

Chapter 3

Team Building at the Top

INTRODUCTION

Parallel to the development of the team as a principal functional unit of organisations runs the development of a myriad of team building interventions offered by consultants, popular books and personnel specialists. However, recent reviews of the effectiveness of team building interventions have shown that while they often have a reliable effect upon team members' attitudes to and perceptions of one another, there is little impact upon team task performance. How do we reconcile the contradiction between the increase in the number of team building interventions offered and the lack of evidence justifying their effectiveness?

It appears that most team building interventions focus on team relationships and cohesiveness, and are based on the mistaken assumption that improvements in cohesiveness lead to improvements in team task performance. In the few interventions which have focused primarily on task issues there does appear to be some improvement in task-related performance, though not consistently so. In this chapter a clear distinction is drawn between team task processes and team social processes.

As has been argued elsewhere in this book, team social processes are unlikely to affect team task processes unless there has been a major breakdown of relationships within the team. What is also emphasised is the value of clarifying the type of team building intervention required and then identifying very specific objectives, rather than assuming that a general intervention will have certain effects. Top management teams require different team building interventions to other teams because of the nature of the task involved (highly complex and strategic) and also because of the composition of such teams (members are usually heads of functions/departments) and how often they get to meet as a team. For many, team building interventions are based on the expectation that a day or two of team building will lead to dramatic improvements in team functioning. It is equivalent to hoping that one session of psychotherapy will change a person's life dramatically. The evidence suggests that it is continual interaction and effort which lead to improvements in functioning rather than any "quick fix".

WHAT IS TEAM BUILDING?

Team building can be described as the "deliberate process of facilitating the evolution of a close and effective work group"[1] so that:

- team leadership is coherent, visionary and acceptable

- the team roles, functions and "deliverables" are clearly understood

- members of the team are emotionally committed and dedicate their efforts to collective achievement

- there is a positive, energetic and empowering climate in the work group

- meetings, both informal and formal, are efficient and make effective use of time and available resources

- weaknesses in team capability have been diagnosed and their negative effects mitigated or eliminated.[2]

KEY QUESTIONS IN TEAM BUILDING

Before committing to a team building intervention, you may be experiencing some reservations. Such reservations are a good thing. Before deciding on a team building activity, the specific needs of the team and the organisation need to be diagnosed so that team building concentrates on what that specific team needs: for example, are the team goals operational/strategic? Are there high levels of certainty/uncertainty? What stage is the group at? Is the group ready for team building? What are their views on the process? Once the needs of the team have been identified and clarified, a suitable team building intervention can be selected. Below are some key questions asked by CEOs when contemplating initiating such a programme.[3]

"I'm uncertain about this team concept. Will it work in our organisation?"

This concern remains an underlying, prevailing theme. It may arise from the fear that management are not fully behind the team endeavour or the notion that team building is simply a fad. This has particular relevance for the senior group as the idea of a senior executive team remains for some executives an elusive concept. Such a belief can have negative repercussions further down the organisation. Pat Cunneen of Analog Devices agrees:

> A particular difficulty is where senior managers do not openly demonstrate teamwork themselves yet expect their respective organisations to work harmoniously in teams. How can junior employees work in the

spirit of teamwork, when all they see above them is internecine warfare?

Team building is not just the latest fad. It is a whole new way of viewing the concept of work. It is a cultural statement which reflects the move from management led, top down, traditional culture to an employee-centered, bottom up approach. Because cultural change is a difficult and slow process, there is bound to be resistance. Indeed, it is through resistance that the real values of team building are discussed.

If resistance is not articulated, it will fester. However, if concerns about team building are expressed, advocates of team work will be forced to present the rationale for team building. The purpose, direction and role of teams will have to be clearly stated and justified. Without resistance, team building can often become an empty exercise, simply put into place because it is the latest organisational buzz word. An effective way to deal with scepticism towards or mistrust of team building is to get it out in the open. Introduce a discourse phase before any decision is made where people can openly discuss their views on team building. Questions asked during this phase will be invaluable in building commitment and providing structure to the whole team building process.

"How long does the team building process take? How much time should the company devote to team building?"

Long-term intervention process is the most effective approach. Although management understand the legitimacy of this in theory, they do not always follow it with commitment. This is one of the biggest obstacles facing effective team building. As mentioned earlier, rapid fire solutions do not work. A day session with a consultant does not "build" a team.

The formal team building process may last 12 to 24 months, with regular intervention from consultants. Team building must be viewed as an ongoing developmental process in order to be effective. It is important for the team not to expect too much in the initial stages.

Key achievements may take time at the beginning (for example structuring a set of operating guidelines that everyone accepts) and the accomplishment of such should be followed by a period of assimilation – to recognise and reinforce one another for their accomplishments and to make necessary adjustments as decisions are implemented. Momentum must not be lost; progression to new goals needs to be encouraged. There will be difficult periods where issues need to be discussed again and again, and reworked. This needs to be addressed and understood from the beginning so that people do not become disillusioned.

Some land mines that may be encountered on the way, as identified by Buck, are: failure to let team members take ownership of an area of responsibility and make the necessary decisions (again, constructive errors should not be punished here); failure to analyse the organisation's policies, procedures and systems to determine whether they are compatible with the concept of team management, learning to give up power and still remain "in charge"; overreaction to mistakes; and dealing with plateaus and boundaries.[4] Such land mines need to be foreseen and planned for.

"What happens when members of the team are difficult to get on with?"

Member relationships is often the biggest worry in teams. Often a comfortable set of relationships and processes is not very practical for a team. It may also be inconsistent with the needs of the team. Teams are made up of diverse skills, backgrounds, areas of expertise and personality types. Because of this variety (if effective team building is in place) the team should be equipped to view problems and make decisions in a synergistic manner. For creativity and innovation to emerge, the right mix is required.

Diversity can also lead to conflict. However, the difficulties and tensions experienced by the team should not be looked upon in a negative light. It needs to be recognised that such diversity is vital to the survival of the team. Often, the most unsettling team member can be one of the most valuable. His or her views may never be fully accepted but exposure to such views may prompt others to consider them and extend their way of thinking. See Chapter 5 for a more in-depth discussion on functional and dysfunctional conflict.

However, there are individuals who are so divisive that they prevent the group coming together as a team. Often, educating people on different personality styles and emphasising the need for diversity is enough. We examine several relationship driven team building interventions later in this chapter. In very extreme cases, and as a last resort, this will not be enough – the decision then is whether some individuals on the team can and should be replaced.

"What is the most important component of effective team building?"

Most theorists and practitioners stress that trust is essential for effective team building. Without trust, creativity is curtailed. Trust is a much discussed but elusive term. Trust must be earned through action. Team discussions and team sharing must be dealt with in confidence at times – if members believe such confidence will be maintained trust is present. There should be open, free flowing debates where members are encouraged to share information that would be beneficial to the group even when such information was previously in their exclusive domain.

There must also be duality of trust. This implies that the team trusts the CEO and the CEO trusts the team. First, team members must trust the intentions of the firm's leadership. The team must believe in management's purpose "to build and empower teams to facilitate organisational outcomes and individual member successes".[5] Secondly, members must trust the behaviour of the CEO. It is not enough that he or she espouses such views as empowerment and consultation; teams have to trust that they will act upon these views. Thirdly, the CEO must trust the team. They must believe the team has the intention (and the skills and talent to carry out this intention) of moving the company towards higher productivity and greater efficiency.

A key component of trust, according to Pat Cunneen of Analog Devices, is the creation of mutual accountability, where the team accepts both individual and group accountability for the achievement of the goal and makes the point that:

> Successful teams support each other and do not behave in a way that simply suggests "well, I did my bit … so it's not my fault if we don't succeed". Mutual accountability also requires people to confront each other in the event of non delivery of commitments in an open and frank manner. This is a particularly important skill as team members may not be experienced in giving constructive feedback, especially to someone who does not work for them.

DIFFERENT TEAM BUILDING INTERVENTIONS

There are many different approaches to team building. Depending on the specific needs of the team, some are more appropriate than others. We now proceed to examine three team-building approaches focusing on (a) purpose,[6] (b) task and (c) relationships.

Emphasis on purpose

The thought behind this approach is that teams have purposes. The team has to interact with other teams and systems to achieve these purposes. This requires a shared vision and commitment to the team purpose by the members. All members need to be engaged in the process. The practical realisation of this could follow the steps below.

The first step is to present a suggested outline of the structure of the workshop, share ideas and suggestions in order to establish a climate of trust and safety. Establish the ground rule of confidentiality. Identify what members want from the workshop. Agree on the needs of the team and come to an agreement about what structure and process will meet those needs.

The second step is to map any influences on your organisation and how these influences are changing. Do this individually and then as a team. List implications for the team. Then map the influences on the team and what the relationships are between individual members and these influences. How do they feel about these influences?

The third step is to map the future. What is the individual member's vision for the organisation and for their role within the organisation? Each member then shares this vision with the team. The next step is to create a purpose from the future vision that all members are committed to.

In order to proceed to the next step, it is worth taking time out to develop listening skills. In theory, this sounds simple but very often, in practice, we are not fully listening to what is being said. Divide into pairs and give equal air time. Practice active listening by using appropriate non-verbal behaviour (maintain eye contact, be relaxed); do not interrupt the speaker; concentrate on what is being said and how it is being said, rather than on what you are going to say next. Ask yourself what is not being said. Paraphrase at the end to ensure understanding.

Pairs then identify the key issues that the team needs to tackle to realise its purpose and share these amongst the team. The group decides on key issues and tackles them. Review of task and process learning follows. This approach can generate powerful insights because of its use of thoughts and feelings, words and maps, and reality and vision. It looks at the process and the relationship behind team building.

The experience of Fergus Barry, Irish Management Institute (IMI), of a purpose driven intervention is a very positive one:

> The most powerful intervention I have witnessed is one where the top team analysed their business environment and then developed a clear vision, purpose and objective. Then each individual produced a document identifying his/her roles and responsibilities. Each individual with a facilitator present then agreed his/her role and responsibilities with his/her manager. Each member then at a team meeting presented his or her responsibilities to the team. This meant that each individuals' roles and responsibilities were in line with the team purpose and objectives and that each team member knew what his/her colleagues were doing.
>
> At the end of this session the group were facilitated in agreeing:
> 1. What they wanted from their colleagues
> 2. What they offered to their colleagues
>
> After this workshop they agreed how they would work together as a team. The team had thus contracted together to achieve team objectives by working together. In psychological terms the team were now (as they say in partnership law) both severally and jointly responsible for the team achieving its objectives.
>
> Each member of the team was then facilitated in giving and receiving

feedback to each of his/her colleagues. I found this the most useful and powerful part of the intervention as it particularly allowed me to identify the behaviours I liked from each of my colleagues and the ones I disliked. It was also invigorating to get the feedback directly from each team colleague with a facilitator present. On a personal note there was one colleague with whom I was having a number of small disagreements. I didn't particularly look forward to this one-to-one session. However, at the session it emerged that there was a lot of respect for the professionalism and personal style of each individual but there were also one or two behaviours that we did not like in each other. After the feedback session it was amazing how we not only worked well together but also became real friends. The initial perceptions when not confronted had stopped the development of the work and personal relationship.

Task driven interventions

In order to deal with specific known problem issues the team must take time out to define carefully the task related problem it is confronting. Then the team develops alternative options for overcoming the problem and action plans for implementing the selected way forward. This can take place within sub-groups who brainstorm for solutions to the problem – each sub-group reports back with a list of suggestions.

Very often, specific problems may only be a symptom of an underlying problem. Introducing a task focused list of unshared assumptions such as those explored overleaf can sometimes help target the real problem. In order to generate open discussion about the team's basic assumptions regarding the task, make a list of statements and get each member to vote on each statement (see Table 3.1). Divide the team into pairs and each pair will report back to the team on how they voted and why. Previously unshared assumptions regarding the task can then be discussed openly by the team.

Where a specific problem can be identified and team members are satisfied they have correctly identified the nature of the problem and not simply a symptom of a deeper unresolved team issue, it is useful to take time out for focused intervention. The content and process of the intervention depends very much on the nature of the problem.

Sometimes the known problem need not concern internal team functioning. The problems may be operational like team X who spent time working with Mike West. This team was responsible for the production of springs used by the Ford motor company. They were experiencing problems with rejection rates from Ford who informed them that the quality of their springs was not up to the standards required. A team meeting was set up to learn techniques of total quality management and continuous improvement from an expert. This led to changes in team objectives, strategies and processes which had a dramatic

Table 3.1: Unshared Assumptions about the Task[7]

1. Standards mean top down control
2. Intuition is unreliable
3. Bottom line is the true judge
4. Logic and facts are king
5. Change is haphazard
6. Why fix what isn't broken?
7. Rules are there to be obeyed
8. Detail equals security
9. To do something, you must first dream that it is possible

impact on quality. The team was subsequently promoted far up the list of Ford's accredited suppliers.

Relationship driven interventions

Relationship driven interventions focus on interpersonal relationships, social support, team climate, support for growth and development of team members, and conflict resolution. They aim to promote a positive social climate and team member well-being.

Interventions should focus on one area rather than attempting to accomplish change in all. If, for example, the main problem is a lack of social support in the team, one solution might be to train team members in simple co-counselling techniques where individuals undertake to give a partner in the team a set period of time – say half an hour or an hour every month – to discuss work-related problems. It is a mutual contract where both team members are provided with equal time at the same session and ensures that all team members get regular support. The basic techniques of co-counselling can be taught at an intervention or on a course.

If the problem relates more to support for growth and development, the team might spend a day identifying each other's skill training or personal development needs and then action plan for how they could best provide the support to enable these needs to be met. General social climate problems can be addressed by asking team members to agree to simple behavioural rules for improving team functioning, such as arranging regular and varied social events. Again action planning and agreed contracting arrangements within the team can promote the likelihood that good intentions will be carried through. Finally, if the problem relates to a failure to resolve conflicts in a timely fashion, conflict resolution techniques based on the principles of assertiveness and ethical negotiation can be introduced. Below is an example of a relationship driven intervention. Here the emphasis is on the validity of feelings. Ask people to listen, describe what people do and what you feel. Do not judge and give feedback with support.

Divide into pairs and share hopes and fears for the event. Again, as mentioned above, listening skills are encouraged. Discuss what you hope to achieve from the intervention and also what you hope for from your team members.

In order to get team members to openly discuss their basic work relationship assumptions, make a list of statements which each pair must discuss (see Table 3.2). Get each individual to "vote" on each assumption as before. Each pair reports back on how they voted and why. Explore the different underlying assumptions of each individual and why they feel that way. Pairs identify areas where the team as a whole or sub-teams are not working well in the light of the shared assumptions.

The team then plans how to improve negative areas – team members need to ensure that the relationship difficulties they have already adopted are still not operating as they do this. Finally, plan for the future and review the event.

Team building emphasising relationships can be useful in top management teams where fragmentation and distrust exist. However, many teams find this area disconcerting: first, it is not a step by step process but an evolving one and secondly, paradoxically, the teams that are most in need of this type of team building are the teams who are most resistant.

However, it is extremely important to work at building positive relationships within teams while ensuring that the "built" teams do not become too cohesive and fall victim to group-think. Such team building exercises can tackle the team's perception of conflict and how to deal with it.

Table 3.2: Unshared Assumptions about Relationships

1.	Team members should get on
2.	I find it difficult to work with people I don't like
3.	Trust is a must
4.	Process is secondary to results
5.	Team building is unnecessary and a waste of time
6.	If I expose my true feelings I will be punished
7.	Bullying and ridicule are part of the give and take of a true team

Another useful exercise is exploring team member satisfaction with the existing team social processes through the use of a simple yet effective questionnaire. Each team member fills out the questionnaire. Have the whole team discuss team scores on this questionnaire and discuss whether there is a need to improve any of those areas of team social functioning.

Table 3.3: Satisfaction with Team Social Processes

	Yes, very definitely	Yes, but only somewhat	No, but only somewhat	No, definitely not
Does the team provide adequate levels of social support for its members?	1	2	3	4
Does the team have constructive, healthy approaches to conflict resolution?	1	2	3	4
Does the team have a generally warm and positive social climate?	1	2	3	4
Does the team provide adequate support for skill development, training and personal development of all its members?	1	2	3	4

The following sections deal with three specific forms of team building interventions: formal reviews, Myers-Briggs Type Indicator (or alternative specialist team building tools) and the value workshop. All three benefit from external expert facilitation. However, the Myers-Briggs programme requires a licensed facilitator.

Regular formal reviews

One team building intervention is that of formal reviews. Formal reviews usually take the form of "away days" of one or two day's duration during which the team reviews objectives, roles, strategies and processes in order to maintain and promote effective functioning.

As in any other area of human activity, regular review of functioning can lead to greater awareness of strengths, skills, weaknesses and problem areas, and future functioning being improved. Whether for individuals, couples, families, teams or organisations, there is value in stepping back from ongoing day-to-day processes, examining areas of activity and reflecting upon the appropriateness of existing ways of doing things. Within work teams, regular away days are a useful way of ensuring a team's continuing effectiveness. Indeed there is much evidence that teams which take time out to review processes are more effective than those which do not.

When should a team take time out for an away day? When a team is involved in completing its work effectively and busy with task-related issues, an away day to review activities can be disruptive. A good time to schedule an away day is when a team has completed a major component of its work. However, if away days are regularly established, for example on a six-monthly basis, then these need not interfere with the team's normal functioning since they are expected and can be used to deal with specific issues identified by the team. Away days should be of at least one full day's duration since there is usually more to talk about than is anticipated. Two days is ideal for most teams, but in some cases, this may be perceived as a luxury.

There is great advantage in conducting away days in comfortable locations away from the team's normal working environment. It is wise to hold team sessions well away from the demands of the place of work to avoid "urgent" interruptions. At the same time, there is much to be said for the kind of comfort and facilities provided in hotels and conference venues. Having a good supply of flip charts, pens, paper, post-it notes, good food and pleasant surroundings can make the team work enjoyable and pleasurable, especially for those who are reluctant initially. Both the financial commitment and the time invested in a well-conducted, focused away day is more than amply remunerated by the returns in performance which can accrue.

All team members should attend away days and, where possible, a facilitator should be commissioned. Facilitators enable team leaders and other team members to focus on the content of the day, without being distracted by responsibility for the processes. Also, a facilitation team can sometimes provide an outside view of processes and comment on apparent diversions or blockages. Facilitators should be chosen with care. They should have experience of team interventions and be knowledgeable about team processes. Ideally the facilitation team will include a chartered occupational psychologist who can provide evidence of team development work in other organisational settings and who would be prepared to give the names of contacts in organisations who could vouch for the effectiveness of their intervention work. The facilitator should have a good knowledge of the relevant research literature on groups at work. Finally, he or she should advise on how to evaluate the effectiveness of the interventions.

Away days must be carefully planned, but with a sufficient degree of flexibility to allow emerging topics to be dealt with appropriately. Having a well-structured programme of activities is essential for a productive away day. It is useful to have a mix of individual work, pairs work, syndicate work and whole group work. Individual work is often necessary to enable team members to clarify their thoughts and reactions to various issues before being exposed to the melting pot of the whole group. Pairs work is an invaluable way of ensuring that all team members are encouraged to be active in the process of reviewing activities. It is also much less threatening for some team members than working in larger groups. Syndicate work involves small sub-groups of the team working together and this can encourage team members who do not normally work together to share their knowledge and expertise. Finally, whole group work is valuable in ensuring that the whole team has ownership of outcomes. It also minimises suspicions about any secret deals and political manoeuvrings which might be taking place.

What topics or what content should be dealt with? There is little value in trying to cover every topic in one day. Changing behaviour is extremely difficult and trying to change complex teams in one session is practicably impossible. Away days should focus on a limited range of topics, such as objectives and communication. One indication that an away day intervention has attempted to cover too many areas is when the end of the day is rushed and action plans are ill-specified and badly formulated.

Topics to be covered in an away day can include:

- team successes and difficulties in the previous six-month or one-year period

- a review of team objectives and their appropriateness

- the roles of team members

- quality of team communication

- team interaction frequency

- team decision-making processes

- excellence in the team's work

- support for innovation

- team social support

- conflict resolution in the team

- support for personal growth and development.

The main thing is to get the team reflecting on their performance as a team, on their objectives and how they intend to achieve those objectives. The following team observation reflexivity rating sheet is an effective way for a facilitator to observe group behaviour when an intact management team is addressing a group task. Feedback on the extent to which those processes are present or absent can represent an important learning experience for the top management team. It is particularly effective when the team is videotaped and illustrative examples discussed during feedback to the team.

Figure 3.1: Team Observation Reflexivity Rating Sheet

Rate the following on a scale 1-5: 1 = no, did not occur, 3 = to a moderate extent, 5 = to a great extent

Task or Meeting Structure:

Did the team: spend time planning the structure of the meeting or task?   1 2 3 4 5
work out the plan in detail before commencing the task?   1 2 3 4 5
include contingencies or alternatives in the plan?   1 2 3 4 5
divide the task into subtasks before commencing?   1 2 3 4 5

Task reflection:

Did the team: question the objectives, strategies or processes for the task?   1 2 3 4 5
review organisational support, or requirements for the task?   1 2 3 4 5
discuss the influence of, or the team response to the environment?   1 2 3 4 5
sustain the reflection during several conversational turns?   1 2 3 4 5
generate alternative objectives, strategies or processes?   1 2 3 4 5
explore the relevance of new techniques, tools, processes to
the task?   1 2 3 4 5
explicitly discuss members' assumptions about the task?   1 2 3 4 5
collectively adopt a new viewpoint or representation of the task?   1 2 3 4 5
try to discover new learnings from reflecting upon the task?   1 2 3 4 5

Team reflection:

Did the team: question the value of its objectives, strategies or processes?   1 2 3 4 5
review organisational support for, or requirements at team level?   1 2 3 4 5
discuss the influence of, or the team response to the environment?   1 2 3 4 5
sustain the reflection during several conversation turns?   1 2 3 4 5
generate alternative objectives, strategies or processes for the team? 1 2 3 4 5
explore the relevance of new or modified team processes?   1 2 3 4 5
explicitly discuss members' assumptions about the team?   1 2 3 4 5
collectively adopt a new viewpoint or representation about
the team?   1 2 3 4 5
try to learn how the team learns through reflection?   1 2 3 4 5

Action:

what is the scale of the planned action or change proposed?   1 2 3 4 5
how novel or different is the proposed action for the team?   1 2 3 4 5
does the team feel the status quo will change because of the action? 1 2 3 4 5
how effective do the team feel the proposed change will be?   1 2 3 4 5

Indicate the time scale for planning applications: Immediate (re. meeting or task)
Short term ☐   Long term ☐

To what extent did all team members engage to a similar degree in the
reflexivity process?   1 2 3 4 5

Did the group complete the task?   Yes ☐ No ☐ Rate the overall reflexivity in the team:

If no, to what extent was it complete: Almost ☐   Low ☐
Partially ☐   Moderate ☐
Deferred ☐   High ☐

USING TEAM BUILDING TOOLS

Another effective team building intervention can be the use of a personal development/team building tool such as the Myers-Briggs Type Indicator (MBTI). The MBTI is based on Jungian theory and explores the different ways people absorb information, how they make decisions with that information, whether they get their energy from their internal or external world and how they orient themselves to the outer world. Such tools can not only help us to reflect on how we take in information and make decisions, but can also help us to understand why others make decisions that are different to ours. Often, conflict can arise because we do not understand where the other person is coming from. The MBTI can help discuss such differences and realise that the "other" way is just as valid. In our experience with top teams, the MBTI proved very effective, increasing levels of self-awareness and also appreciation of other team members preferences. As one participant put it:

> Having completed the MBTI , I discovered that I was an ESTJ. I now have an awareness that I could be overcritical, lack empathy and have difficulty motivating others. As an engineer the STJ traits were invaluable, as a manager they are a liability with respect to relationships. The second implication was knowing that a downside of a sensing type was not seeing the big picture, of making connections in disparate information and in being innovative.

> Manager, food company

While the MBTI can only be administered by a trained professional, there are many other inventories that are just as effective. For example Belbin's Team Role Inventory or Cattel's 16 personality factor questionnaires are widely available.

Conducting a values workshop[8]

This workshop aims to generate a discussion to resolve conflict between personal values and those of their team/organisation. This is effective, especially when a team has certain values it feels are espoused but not acted on. It also demonstrates that the leader is taking team values seriously.

Step 1: defining personal values

Because people have different personal values, this can quickly highlight how many different priorities can exist. Each team member engages in what consultants Dennis Jaffe and Cynthia Scott call a Personal Values Exploration, where they sort their personal values into very important, important, less important. They may experience difficulty in categorising their values – they should try to think of specific examples of how each value applies to their lives. It is likely that if they cannot think of specific examples, then the value is not a high priority.

Step 2: sharing values with the team

After participants have ranked their values, they then share them with the team. Each person puts their values on a flipchart. Members then walk around the room, looking at other team members' values. Each participant then chooses someone with values similar to their own and discuss those values. The goal is for people to clarify which goals are central to their work.

Step 3: creating a team values credo

Individuals now come together to define their shared values. The goal of this step is to come up with a statement of shared values on how they want to work together as well as the values for achieving organisational and team goals.

In this step, each participant selects five values from their list that they want expressed at work. Then, they take turns reading their number one (most important value), which a facilitator records on the flipchart. If the value is already on the chart, the facilitator puts a tick beside it.

Members then list the values in descending order of importance – from the one with the most ticks to those with none. What the team have now is a prioritised list of team values.

Step 4: creating a charter of team values

The team list should now generate team discussion. Discussion can revolve around values that aren't expressed frequently enough or are neglected in times of crises. Specific behavioural examples of values might be highlighted or ways identified in which values can be practiced within the team. The potential for discussion is endless but in order for it to be meaningful, there needs to be trust and safety within the group.

ROLE CLARIFICATION AND NEGOTIATION

One potential problem in teams is lack of clarity about team roles. The steps in role clarification and negotiation are described more fully overleaf.

Table 3.4: Role Negotiation Exercise

Role negotiation exercise
Team members use mutual influence and negotiation in order to change team behaviours and improve team functioning.

Step 1
Each team member lists his or her objectives and principal activities on a piece of flip chart paper.

Step 2
Each piece of flip chart paper is hung on the wall around the room and team members examine each role.

Step 3
Under three headings on a piece of paper, each team member writes down what behaviours they would like that person to *do less, do more,* or *maintain at the present level* in their working relationship. For example, one team member might indicate that they need more information/time from another team member to keep them informed more fully of plans for the coming month. Another team member may request full participation at team meetings. Other suggestions may concern frequency and type of communication with the team, prioritising training in "people" skills, discussing the issue of accountability within the team and so on.

Each person signs their name after their requests for more, less or maintained behaviour.

Step 4
Pairs of individuals within the team then meet to examine the end result. The two negotiate together in order to reach agreement about the various requests. This is a highly participative step in the exercise and some teams may need help in managing the negotiation, especially if a particular pair is having difficulty reaching agreement.

Through role negotiation, the needs of individual roles are met more effectively and the functioning of individual members is dovetailed more into the objectives and needs of the team as a whole. This is a very powerful exercise which can enhance team functioning considerably, overcoming many of the problems of process loss and coordination.

RETHINKING TEAM BUILDING

Team building involves two sides. On the positive side, participants get the opportunity to get together and enjoy team building sessions in a relaxed and informal manner. However, a darker side to the process can emerge, where team members face such negative emotions as fear, shame, guilt and hopelessness, when their motives and behaviour are assessed.[9]

Though such emotions feel threatening, they are imperative to the success of ongoing team building. However, before the darker side of team building can be put to positive use, three myths associated with teamwork should be debunked.[10] First, the myth that it is imperative to stay positive in order for team building to be successful – sometimes it is necessary to explore unpleasant realities in order to function more effectively as a team. This cannot be done if team members feel it would be inappropriate to express negativity or the confidentiality of the session is in question. Secondly, there exists a misconception that resistance needs to be overcome at all times – this is not necessarily the case. Resistance can have a positive effect in that it leads to open discussion, justifying certain decisions and exploration of hidden assumptions. The third and final myth is that being too personal is counterproductive. Again, this is not necessarily the case. Openly expressing personal views and emotions can be positive if voiced in the right environment, in an appropriate manner. The aim of this chapter has been to provide different possibilities to do this.

Activities and exercises on the positive side of team building are designed to generate trust and openness within the group. People have the chance to get acquainted outside the work environment. However, because team building is more than a series of playful activities, there are aspects of team building that people may find difficult. It is a process where participants experience trust and willingness to explore core issues that are crucial to the successful functioning of the team. This is not always pleasant or simple.

CONCLUSION

This chapter has emphasised the need for teams to review their functioning on a regular basis. Where a team is low in task reflexivity it is necessary to address this failure of adaptability. Some members of the team fear that such questioning generates conflict and uncertainty about the team's direction. However, it is important to reassure team members that such reflexivity holds within it the seeds of opportunity and greater effectiveness which can produce an enhanced sense of competence, confidence and greater aspirations amongst team members. Moreover, the research evidence on reflexivity has strongly suggested that teams which do reflect on strategies in this way are highly effective in long-term performance. Reflexivity should, therefore, not simply involve team building interventions, it should be part of the texture of the day-to-day life of the team.

The different approaches to team building interventions have been examined and it has been stressed that teams should adopt interventions appropriate to their particular purposes. The blanket approach to team building often employed is unlikely to be effective for most teams. The first question to ask is, "What intervention is most appropriate, for which teams and at which point in time?" Then the following checklist can be used to ensure appropriate focus for the intervention:

1. Are the objectives of the intervention clear?

2. Is the intervention appropriate for the particular issues facing the team?

3. Is the intervention appropriately timed?

4. Does the intervention attempt to cover too many areas?

5. Are means for sustaining change built in to the intervention?

6. Are facilitators employed who have the knowledge and skills required to conduct team building interventions?

7. Will clear action plans emerge as a result of the team building intervention?

8. Will regular reviews be instituted as a result of the team building intervention?

We now turn to the central issue of leading the top management team.

Chapter 4

CEO Leadership and the Top Management Team

The required leadership style is that of the cultivator. In the original horticultural analogy of company culture, the cultivator marked out and prepared the ground and sowed the seeds. Nature did the rest. But nature cannot be forced; it can be harnessed or worked with – cultivated-but not forced. Likewise, in the new economy, strategic leaders will mark out the themes, sow the seed and then let nature – tacit and interactive knowledge – do the rest. The emerging description of such organisations as "communities of practice" comes close to capturing the essence of these new organisational forms.

Charles Carroll, IMI

INTRODUCTION

In the 21st century, organisational leaders face an increasingly complex task. Globalisation and the rapid diffusion of information and communication technologies (ICT) are transforming economies, organisations and the nature of work itself. In the knowledge era, the driving force of employment, innovation and growth is intellectual capital. Occupations with a high information and knowledge content have become increasingly central to economic activity. As organisations shift the central focus of their competitive strategy away from value appropriation towards value creation, it is the leader who can elicit the untapped value adding potential of all employees who will prosper in the new millenium.

To compete in the information age, organisations must increasingly harness the knowledge, skills, experience, attitudes and networks of all their employees in order to assimilate and create the new knowledge required to fuel innovation and new product development. The role of the CEO within the top management group and the wider organisation is a crucial factor in this process. CEOs must act as leaders of learning in the 21st century and must harness the collective wisdom and imagination of TMG members, core knowledge workers and front line employees engaged in service delivery. Crafting an imaginative and engaging mission is a crucial element in this leadership process.

Without an imaginative mission it becomes very difficult for the CEO to inspire followers. This is because the job of persuasion, which faces every CEO, is made easier when followers can relate, at both an emotive and cognitive level, to the implementation challenges set out in the mission statement. As the Japanese proverb puts it "vision without action is a daydream; action without vision is a nightmare". In addition to the capacity to envision others, leaders also need the skills to manage a team high in participatory involvement and they must actively foster an organsiational culture to support this. The capacity to manage external constituencies, change and support innovation are core areas of competence for the modern day leader. Four main leadership styles have been identified.[1] These are the laissez-faire leader, the authoritarian leader, the transactional leader and the transformational leader. Of all the different types of leaders, we believe that it is the transformational leader who is most suited to fulfilling these diverse and sometimes conflicting roles.

LAISSEZ-FAIRE LEADERSHIP

This type of leader exists where there is an absence of leadership in a person who holds a position of responsibility. This leader shows very little initiative and rarely attempts to influence others. A lack of vision, goals and perform-ance expectations typify the non-leader. The followers have no clear direction or vision to follow. They may be disoriented due to confusion over the goals they are supposed to achieve and the level of performance expected from them.

AUTHORITARIAN LEADERSHIP

The authoritarian leaders rely on their formal position of authority for power. They establish and assign goals for the subordinates in a directive manner. Their behaviour is characterised by commands, instructions and non-contingent reprimand (chiding subordinates for reasons not directly related to performance). Followers rarely offer initiative and tend not to question the wisdom or commands of the leader. Such leaders have an imbalance of power in the management teams that they lead which can lead to distrust among the team members. The presence of the autocratic CEO has been found to impair decisions, as other team members tend not to assert their positions.[2] It has also been found that the resultant power centralisation can lead to high levels of politics, distrust between members and internal competition for the attention of the leader. While the vast majority of CEOs in the Irish software industry interviewed felt this style of leadership was not characteristic of how they led, one or two identified with certain elements of being an authoritarian leader. One CEO felt there was too much emphasis on interpersonal relationships and being a team player. When asked if he would describe his senior management group as a team, he responded with the following statement:

> Team? I don't know and to be honest, I don't particularly care. I don't have the time to be worrying about whether we are a team or not. As long as I get results, I'm satisfied.

TRANSACTIONAL LEADERSHIP

Transactional leaders view themselves as supplying all the wisdom (in terms of vision, strategy and goals) in the organisation. They use the issue of subordinate rewards to gain and maintain power. Followers comply with the leader's wishes when their desires are met by rewards. The leader expresses confidence in the subordinate's ability to attain high levels of performance. The leader provides contingent personal rewards, contingent material rewards and expresses dissatisfaction through contingent reprimand. Followers are in a position resembling more of a partnership than in the previous leadership styles. However, because the relationship between leader and follower is one based on exchange, where the follower's needs are met if their performance meets expectations – the follower's concerns can become focused on immediate self-interest rather than the good of the team/organisation.

TRANSFORMATIONAL LEADERSHIP

> The task of the CEO is no longer to be the font of wisdom, but rather an enabler who ensures that the conditions for continually developing responsiveness are maintained
>
> Michael Shiel, IMI

Of all the leadership styles discussed, transformational leadership is the most effective when leading under conditions of high uncertainty, knowledge intensity and change because it focuses on the leader's effect on the followers. Transformational leadership inspires trust, loyalty, respect, high levels of motivation and independence of thinking. Bass, one of the most important writers on transformational leadership, emphasises the importance of charisma, intellectual stimulation, the ability to inspire and motivate followers, and the provision of personal support.[3]

Charisma and the transformational leader

Charisma for the ancient Greeks meant "divinely inspired gift". Over the years, it is a word that has been increasingly used to describe exceptional leaders.

Terms such as heroic, charismatic and visionary have been used interchangeably to describe leaders who have profound and lasting effects on their followers. Charismatic leaders arouse strong emotions in their followers and identification with their leader. However, there is a darker side to charismatic leadership that can lead to the leader's downfall. Bass maintains that while "charisma is a necessary ingredient of transformational leadership, by itself, it is not sufficient to account for the transformational process".[4]

In order to be a transformational leader, one does not need to inspire devotion and personal loyalty. A transformational leader is looking for commitment to ideas, not a group of acolytes. While the darker side of charismatic leadership can lead to dependency and disciples, transformational leadership produces followers who can think for themselves but who are committed to the same vision.

In advocating charisma as an integral component of transformational leadership, Bass is not referring to a leader as showman or celebrity but rather the ability to build a vision and arouse others to follow that vision. The ability to inspire emotion and commitment to that vision amongst followers is an integral element of the transformational leader's repertoire.

Followers are also regarded as an inspirational source of wisdom and direction. They become self-leaders due to a sense of emotional commitment and ownership to the challenging goals set by the transformational leader. These leaders nurture self-development and self-reliance. Behaviour exhibited includes: encouraging self-goal-setting, encouraging self-monitoring of performance, creating positive thought patterns and developing reward structures that support self-leadership. This is very different from the charismatic leader who inspires, and demands, blind devotion and dependency.

The transformational leader is well suited to industries where intellectual capital and knowledge employees provide the source of competitive advantage.

Intellectual stimulation and transformational leadership

Another type of behaviour identified by Bass as being integral to the transformational leader is the ability to increase both the leaders' and the followers' awareness of problems and to view problems from several different perspectives. Linked to this is the leader's ability to effectively manage cognitive complexity.

Leaders must be attuned to perceiving conspicuous trends in the environment. They need the cognitive ability to process widely different types of information and to be capable of judging accurately the direction in which the environmental forces are directed. Studies have shown that those who become organisational leaders are, in general, better adapted than most to deal with cognitive complexity. They are able to filter through information to obtain what they need; they are capable of making sense of an ever increasingly complex environment and then in using the data obtained in problem-solving. Manfred Kets de Vries maintains that managing cognitive complexity manifests itself in simplification, the ability to make complex and ambiguous issues manageable.[5] He cites Carlo de Benedetti of Olivetti and Percy Barnevik of ABB as examples of leaders who successfully manage cognitive complexity. It also implies being comfortable with ambiguity and paradox – sometimes described as the capacity to manage polarities. Such paradoxes or tensions include the struggle between stability and change; the struggle between being a manager and being a leader;[6] fostering trust in an increasingly competitive environment; and balancing internal and external tensions. Perhaps, one of the biggest challenges facing the CEO today is that which Michael Shiel at IMI refers to as "the task of engaging the organisation in a conversation which maintains the drive and momentum of the firm but does not dissipate the individual member's drive or imagination".

However, the above behaviours are not enough in themselves. If the transformational leader has a vision but does not provide the support to achieve it, then the vision will remain elusive. If the leader advocates intellectual risk taking but there is a lack of mutual trust in the organisation, then individual knowledge will never be translated into organisational learning. Charisma and intellect are not enough to lead through transformation. The ability of the leader to provide personal support in an open and trusting environment requires self-awareness and the ability to inspire trust and motivation through the management of meaning.

SELF-AWARENESS

Self-awareness is at the core of all the skills necessary for effective leadership mentioned above. It is necessary to understand what it is that makes you behave in certain ways in order to alter behaviour for the better. Not being aware of how you feel in the world of work means you may lack sufficient information to make effective decisions, which can be very detrimental. For example, the inability to understand and defuse anger in the workplace can lead to reoccurring and unresolved conflicts amongst employees, poor morale and a fall in productivity. The emotional or intuitive processes are rarely nurtured within organisational life. However, more and more executives are realising the need for both emotional and business acumen. After all, much of the behaviour within organisations is based on emotions, many of which are defensive and negative in nature.

Management scholars such as Chris Argyris at Harvard University have identified how the actions of many middle and senior managers engage in defensive mechanisms based on fear, anxiety and mistrust, designed to protect and further their own self-interests.[7]

To eradicate such defensive behaviour, self-awareness is crucial. A CEO needs to be aware that he or she also engages in defensive routines. It requires courage to examine how you react to people and events in work. Larry Ellison, CEO of Oracle believes that self-knowledge is vital to achieving your full potential. This involves being aware of your strengths and weaknesses and surrounding yourself with individuals who will not hesitate to tell you when you are making a mistake. This necessity was demonstrated by Lee Iacocca when he frankly assessed his strengths and weaknesses in a television interview with NBC news.[8] It also takes courage and honesty. Larry Ellison maintains it often means

> possessing the combination of humility and arrogance. One without the other will rob you of your potential. You have to have the confidence to really stretch yourself – see what you can do. On the other hand, you can't deceive yourself so thoroughly and be so brash and rude that you can't work as part of a team. You need the combination.[9]

The emotional intelligence expert Daniel Goleman[10] identifies five building blocks necessary for increased self-awareness:

• emotional awareness – knowing one's emotions and intentions

• self-regulation – managing one's emotions

• motivation – directing one's emotions towards the achievement of a goal

• empathy – recognising emotions in others

• understanding relationships.

Mike Fiszer, a management development specialist at the Irish Management Institute, is keenly aware in his role as a leadership coach of the importance of knowing yourself and emotional intelligence. He has found that what many people mistake as the elusive quality of charisma is in fact simply a knowledge and understanding of one's character and the ability to act in character in all situations. Leadership, he stresses, is not tailoring your style for every situation so much as knowing who you are and living consistently with who you are. Warren Bennis, the best selling leadership author and former University President, refers to this as "constancy".[11]

This may often involve confronting one's inner fears and testing one's capabilities. Mike Fiszer uses the metaphor of a diver on a diving board to illustrate this point. A diver climbs on to the first board and dives off, he climbs on the second board, looks down, makes a judgement and dives. He climbs on the third board, braces himself and makes the leap. On the fourth board, he realises his limitations – what does he do? Does he go ahead and dive anyway, does he jump and hope for the best? Or does he turn around, facing those behind him and converse with them? It is the last option that can be the most frightening to many leaders and it is the last option that demonstrates self-awareness. Facing others and facing your own limitations.

An effective leader is not an individual who appears flawless – it is an individual who knows him/her self well enough to know not only their strong points, but also their weak points. Indeed John Hunt at London Business School believes that a flaw can have the effect of creating a sense of humanity amongst the followers.[12] It is this leader who will seek to work on their deficiencies but, often more importantly, to identify team members who are strong in the leader's area of weakness. Such openness can be uncomfortable, however, and many leaders engage in defensive mechanisms in order to avoid confronting their areas of weaknesses. In order to openly address our weaknesses as well as our strengths it is imperative that there exists a duality of trust.

While self-awareness is being identified by both practitioners and academics as being integral to effective leadership, it is a difficult and often threatening experience. Michael Shiel of the IMI emphasises that there are many different levels of self-awareness and that it is infinite how deep you can go. He identifies three approaches to self-awareness, each level leading to higher levels of self-awareness: the instrumental approach, the reflective approach and the case-in-point approach.

The instrumental approach

This is the most frequently used approach and involves the use of instruments such as 360 degree feedback and Myers-Briggs Type Indicator. Such instruments usually involve a self-report questionnaire and in the case of 360 degree feedback, feedback from peers, direct reports and supervisors is also included.

How the instruments are administered is critical to the process. Michael Shiel stresses that the real issues at this level are the context the test is administered in and how it is introduced:

> Leaving the questionnaire on the respondents desk simply will not work. The instrument needs to be administered and followed up by a skilled facilitator in a safe environment. Under the right circumstances, these tools can be effective at opening up dialogue and increasing self awareness.

The reflective approach

This approach involves a deeper level of self-exploration. Michael Shiel outlines this process below:

> This approach aims to achieve a higher level of self awareness than the instrumental approach, and therefore I strongly emphasise the need for a safe environment and a skilled facilitator. A facilitator who has good intentions or will tell their own war stories is not enough as the skills required here are very different.

This approach involves small "stranger groups" (groups where people do not know each other). Each group member is asked to reflect on a critical event, for example a situation where they attempted to exercise leadership and did not succeed in doing so. Participants are asked to speculate on why this happened but to resist coming to any conclusions.

All groups come together for a plenary discussion where individuals are invited to share some of their reflections and insights with the group. This exercise can be very powerful if there is trust within the group and skilled facilitation.

Case-in-point approach

The third approach is the most difficult and the most powerful. It requires reflecting on what is happening in the here and now. Michael Shiel describes the process in this way:

> The case-in-point approach requires the individual to focus on working in the moment. The facilitator needs to bring the learning experience into what is happening at that point in time. The facilitator assists the group in understanding what is happening at any given moment as a way of understanding similar situations at work. Anything that happens in the meeting is available for learning. This learning can be transferred to their actions in the organisational context. This approach is used to great effect in the United States in programmes such as the leadership program at the Kennedy School at Harvard University, and at the doctoral program in leadership at the University of San Diego.

This approach is not yet mainstream but because of its powerful results and the high instance of transferability of skills, we expect the technique to grow in popularity. Again, it should be stressed that highly skilled facilitation is crucial. Such a technique demonstrates how blurred the boundaries between formal learning and real applied work settings are.

TRUST MANAGEMENT

> The overheads of distrusting or wary relationships are enormous.
>
> Michael Hammer, Business Strategist

> If there is no sense of trust in the organisation, if people are preoccupied with protecting their backs … creativity will be one of the first casualties.
>
> Manfred Kets de Vries, INSEAD, France

The word trust is defined as the "absolute certainty in the trustworthiness of self or another and it is built and maintained on a foundation of appropriate and honest disclosure, believability and credibility ... and depends first and foremost on making emotional contact with the listener".[13] A lack of trust will lead to misinterpretation, confused communications, cynicism, lack of commitment and goodwill.

Trust and the management group

One of the most fatal mistakes is to construct a top team comprised of executives who replicate the CEO's strengths and weaknesses. At least part of the role of the senior management group is to fill the gaps and offset the weaknesses of the CEO. Therefore, it is imperative that there is trust between the CEO and the top management team. Chancellor Kenneth Shaw, President of Syracuse University, maintains that trust between the senior executives and the CEO is crucial. In his view every CEO has blind spots – the important thing is that the CEO is aware of them and positions experts that he or she can trust to deal with these blind spot areas. Therefore, a well-balanced team requires a CEO who has a high level of self-awareness and also builds trust within the team. However, in reality, such teams are difficult to find:

> The managing director in my organisation finds it very hard to trust anybody; he therefore is threatened by someone who complements his blind spots. This is a big failing in leadership in my company.

> Manager, insurance industry

Trust within the senior management team was cited as being one of the most important factors by CEOs participating in our current study of high technology companies in the software and telecoms industry. Trust within the team was seen as invaluable in order to allow members to express uncertainty, voice concerns and offer constructive criticism. However, while most CEOs were aware of the importance of trust within the TMT, they were all too aware of the difficulties in achieving high levels of trust.

Building trust does not happen overnight and is often quite an unnatural process. People find it difficult to trust one another and this is accentuated when working in a fast paced competitive environment. However, such competitive and often individualistic environments are where trust is most needed. In order to manage this dilemma, the CEO needs to explicitly demonstrate trust for the team and advocate trust as an organisational value. This sometimes means taking risks. In working with top management teams, an exercise we found effective in demonstrating just how tenuous trust can be is the prisoners dilemma. This exercise is designed to create conflict and suspicion through separating groups and blocking off communication. In the vast majority of cases, the exercise leads to breakdown of trust and betrayal, demonstrating how necessary communication and interaction are in maintaining trust.

However, in order to gain trust, actions must also be based on respect for followers. While tough action might sometimes be required, Max de Pree, former CEO of Herman Miller, the US furniture manufacturer and retailer, argues that it is necessary at times to be willing to appear vulnerable and to demonstrate a willingness to trust and depend on the abilities of other people.[14] If trust is present, however, there will be a significant improvement in group effectiveness, quality of decision making and a decrease in defensive behaviour.

While the cognitive brain sifts through factual data, the emotional brain is always scanning for meaning from tone, gestures, eye contact and other behaviours that are outside the cognitive brain's domain. It is very important that what you say matches up to what you do. This can be seen when body language conflicts with the spoken word (for example sometimes detected by the non-verbal behaviour of scratching the nose or lack of eye contact) and also when actions contradict what has been verbalised. An effective leader pays attention to the importance of followers' intuitive powers and engages in what Warren Bennis describes as the management of trust. In order to gain trust, it is important that what the leader is broadcasting is real and genuine. If not, the follower will distrust the message. Mike Fiszer at the IMI believes it would be a mistake as a leader to underestimate our more intuitive powers. He maintains that we all possess quite skilled intuitive pattern systems to detect threatening situations and that a leader who is not genuine or lacks integrity will soon be found out. To gain trust, he advocates being true to yourself. Do not give an answer if you do not have one – but do give what he terms "unrigidly defined areas of certainty". A leader who gains the trust of others is someone who can allow people to "live today while being uncertain of tomorrow".

In order to gain trust, there should be congruence between words, voice, body language and action. The important factor here is credibility. If a manager encourages participation, yet rebukes an individual for supporting an opposing idea, they have lost credibility. Once this is gone, it can take a long time to regain. And without trust, no amount of rhetoric, rituals or slogans will inspire people towards the vision.

INSPIRATIONAL MOTIVATION

> The job of leadership today is not just to make money: it's to make meaning.
>
> John Seely Brown, Xerox[15]

A vision must be transmitted by inspiration, not coercion, and trust in the leader is a prerequisite. In order to communicate the vision, the leader will often use symbolism, metaphors, rituals, mantras and myths. Impression management, "the process by which people attempt to control or manipulate the reactions of others to images of themselves or their own ideas",[16] is an important dimension of the CEO's organisational life. Impression management is nothing new. In nearly all our transactions, social, professional or otherwise, we engage in what Martin describes as "mutual perception".[17] The people we interact with are attempting to influence the impressions we form of them just as we are attempting to control their perceptions of us.

This intentional manipulation of "self information" is generally engaged in to highlight positive aspects and downplay the negative ones. While impression management is sometimes, without doubt, used in a deceptive manner and can have negative consequences, some degree of impression management is necessary in order to maintain social order. For a CEO faced with the ever-expanding pressure to determine the strategic moves of others and to maintain their own positive image, impression management is a necessary tool. There are different impression management techniques, for example, the management of physical appearance or the management of behaviour. A CEO needs to be aware of the importance of *looking* the part – as one US CEO said to the authors "I was faced with the choice of discarding my flares, shaping up and moving up or keeping my dress sense – and moving no-where."

There is also the use of language and rhetoric. While a successful leader does not need to excel in showmanship or theatre, they do need to know the importance of language. Warren Bennis refers to this as the management of meaning and maintains that one of the main differences between Ronald Regan ("the great communicator") and Jimmy Carter was Regan's use of metaphors which people identified with.

According to the University of Limerick and University of Maryland research on top teams, 58 per cent of top team members in US multinationals based in Ireland felt strongly that their CEO was a transformational leader.[18] Most of the CEOs interviewed in our current study of companies in the indigenous software industry felt that this type of leadership was most suited to their industry (high tech, high complexity, high uncertainty). Because human capital is the main competitive advantage of these companies, the leadership required is one of empowerment, where open debate is encouraged. Some CEOs went on to state that they were putting in place explicit conflict stimulation and conflict resolution techniques.

However, such a fast changing industry does pose some very real problems. One CEO mentioned that the high demand and high monetary value attached to IT employees can create managerial problems. He stated that "it can be difficult managing a group who are very aware that demand heavily outweighs supply – in such an industry, trust and commitment are imperative to get people to go that extra mile."

Another CEO mentioned that, despite working with highly qualified experts, many of the problems are not unique to this industry:

> Managing egos is something that the CEO has to do in every industry –
> an effective leader will be aware of insecurities and tensions and will
> deal with them in an emotionally intelligent manner – this means not
> flying off the handle.

The ability to empathise in situations where individuals are uncertain or threatened has been found to make a difference to team cohesiveness which has been demonstrated to impact return on investment and sales growth.[19] Research has also found that teams performing under a high achieving leader perform less effectively than teams performing under an average achieving leader. The main differentiator was found to be the ability to empathise – high achievers are less likely to delegate and set themselves high goals that often result in the alienation of team members.

MANAGING THE TEAM AND ORGANISATIONAL CULTURE

Management of the team

Regardless of the formal structure of an organisation, there will be differences in the extent to which strategic leadership is actually shared among senior executives.[20] In organisations where the CEO adopts an autocratic leadership style, other executives may have little or no say in strategic decisions. In contrast to this, the transformational leader works very closely with the senior team. This type of leader encourages high levels of participation and involvement in all strategic decisions and fosters an environment of support. As discussed earlier, prerequisites for such an environment are trust and safety within the team.

Trust is perhaps one of the most over used words in management today. While it is often advocated, it is rare to find teams that fully trust each other. Perhaps it is unrealistic to strive for total trust in top management teams. Because of different power dynamics, personal goals and agendas and basic human nature, it is difficult for individuals to be totally trusting of each other – and perhaps total trust is not necessary. What is necessary, however, is that there is a mutuality of respect within the team and the members are committed to working towards high levels of trust within the team. A CEO can facilitate this in a practical way. Frequency of interactions between the senior team members has been found to increase knowledge of the different perspectives of team members, increase openness and, in the long term, increase levels of trust. The type of interactions will also affect the functioning of the team. Whereas formal, well-structured meetings have high levels of clarity, the truth sometimes fails to emerge. It is only after the meeting, in the corridor or over coffee that people express their real opinions – citing political complications or personal disputes as the *real* reason a certain strategy will not work. Less formal gatherings might be less structured and less clear but they sometimes elicit very important information that might never be voiced in more formal surroundings. Increased frequency of interaction between top executives and a combination of formal and informal styles can improve participation levels of the top management team.

Increasing levels of participation and involvement of senior team members can be time consuming. In a dynamic and turbulent environment, time is a precious commodity. In a study conducted by Eisenhardt it was found that decisions were faster when the CEO sought advice widely but relied more on a few executives who had the most relevant expertise and experience.[21] Also, decisions were faster when the CEO emphasised the need among the executives most affected by the decision rather than prolonging the process by attempting to achieve total consensus. Depending on the decision to be made and the expertise required, different team members will be more involved than others.

In order to maintain high levels of participation and involvement, it is necessary to promote an organisational culture that will facilitate this process. We will now explore the importance of organisational culture and the role of the CEO in managing it.

CULTURAL RELATIVITY: NETWORK, MERCENARY, FRAGMENTED AND COMMUNAL CULTURES

It is imperative that the CEO understands the organisational culture. If the CEO wishes to foster trust and openness, it is necessary to create a culture that nurtures feelings of self-esteem, participation, empowerment and effectiveness. The CEO needs to be aware that often psychological defences exist in the organisational structures and operating routines that may protect organisational members from feelings of threat or stress and should discuss such defensive actions openly. If there is a lack of congruence between management style and the culture of the organisation, such defensive action will only accentuate sources of endemic conflict.

Rob Goffee and Gareth Jones, of London Business School and Henley Management College respectively, identified four separate typologies of organisational culture using two key dimensions – sociability and solidarity.[22] Sociability is a measure of ordinary friendliness within the organisation, while solidarity is based on the extent to which common task interdependence exists and shared goals operate. Using these dimensions they have identified the following different cultures:

- Network – high on sociability, low on solidarity
- Mercenary – low on sociability, high on solidarity

- Fragmented – low on sociability, low on solidarity
- Communal – high on sociability, high on solidarity.

Additionally, each culture may possess either negative or positive attributes. Each type of dominant culture will require particular skill repertoires on the part of the leader. In the following sections we briefly outline the main features of each culture, focusing on the communal culture in particular. Research conducted on corporate culture with our MBA students has illustrated a strong link between organisational effectiveness, transformational leadership and the communal corporate culture.

The NETWORK culture

High sociability, Low solidarity

The network culture is often defined as a culture of friendship and assistance. The high levels of sociability suggest an emphasis on relationships and trust. There is high value placed on loyalty and trust. However, there can be negative aspects to this culture. The culture of friendship can sometimes mean poor performance will be tolerated. Because everyone knows each other and there is a strong emphasis on the cohesion of the group, it is often difficult to give criticism where it is needed. This can mean that there is very little differentiation between strong and weak performers, leading to feelings of frustration for the strong performers. At its most dysfunctional, network cultures can disintegrate into heavy politicking, with groups forming cliques against one another.

The MERCENARY culture

Low sociability, High solidarity

This culture emphasises performance – regardless of how it is attained. Work, not relationships, is the important factor; social interaction is considered a waste of time unless pursued in the line of business. Conversation is work focused with the bias towards action. Such companies tend to have clear competitive enemies and engage in benchmarking, comparison and set clear specific targets.

Because the focus is on work, feedback is given openly – and without malice. Members are happy to give and receive criticism without it turning personal. There are high comfort levels surrounding conflict and debate.

However, on the negative side, there is a risk that this culture can become too target oriented. When targets are all that people think about, members may stop at nothing to achieve them. In the negative form, such a culture is ruthless and without loyalty. People who do not deliver are eliminated and it becomes a dog eat dog environment. Such organisations may focus on solely short-term goals – "I'll achieve my goals and damn the others!!". Organisational goals are lost in the pursuit for individual goals. Because mistakes will not be tolerated, creativity and life long learning are at a minimum.

The FRAGMENTED culture

Low sociability, Low solidarity

The fragmented culture is characterised by low sociability and low solidarity. This means that members of fragmented organisations are not particularly interested in forming relations at work, nor do they particularly support the institution. They may work *in* the company but they work *for* themselves. This may sound as if there is no positive aspect to such a culture but, like all the others, the fragmented culture has both positive and negative aspects.

In the positive aspect, the individual is judged on performance and quality – no more no less. In such an organisation, there is an emphasis on creativity with little or no fear of offending with criticism. The emphasis here is on ideas not appearance so, there is no obligation to spend time on socialising or politics. Because the focus is on the quality of output, there is a high degree of flexibility and privacy. Examples of this culture in the positive aspect would be newsrooms or university. Here, the focus is on the story or the publication, not the amount of time spent in the office.

In the negative, this culture can be one of the most dysfunctional. Warning signs are pervasive cynicism regarding the organisation, difficulty in recruiting high quality staff and excessive backbiting between members. Especially in knowledge based organisations, when this culture veers into the negative, there is a tendency to knock the ideas of others. The atmosphere is one of superiority and competitiveness with little identification with the organisation.

The COMMUNAL culture

High sociability, High solidarity

This company values both performance and the relationship between the performers. It is a culture of openness and creativity and favours the metaphor of the family.

There is meaningful interest in process and a strong concern for results; members take pride in their product or service. There is a strong focus on the symbolic in such companies where legacies, stories, rituals and symbols are used to heighten members identity with the company. There is usually a strong identification with the company, for example, "the HP way", where members feel proud to be associated with the brandname or logo. There is high loyalty and members tend to work hard and play hard.

Like all cultures, there is a negative side to the communal culture. Such loyalty to the company can mean it takes over your life, with members spending all of their working and leisure time with their co-workers. Often, the feeling of brotherhood and belongingness can lead to complacency and smugness within the company which can in turn lead to group-think.

Leadership in the communal culture

Leaders in the positive communal culture are usually visionaries and highly charismatic. They are aware of the symbolic significance of leadership and are skilled at managing meaning. Examples of symbolic behaviours might include random management by walking around meeting employees on the ground or by taking time out to visit an ill employee. Such symbolic gestures can be reinforced by the use of storytelling and myth. For example, stories about Richard Branson's parachuting journey or his financing of an air stewardess' business idea heard briefly while flying to the UK serve to engender the notion of him as daring and a risk taker. Another example would be Lee Iacocca. During his early years at Chrysler Corporation, he accepted a single dollar as salary for a whole year during the height of the Chrysler crisis. This enormous gesture promoted confidence in the employees and inspired commitment. There is a strong link between transformational leadership and the creation of a positive communal culture.

However, this culture too can foster dysfunctional leaders. In the negative form of this culture the darker side of the charismatic leader is in evidence and symbolic gestures are used to manipulate employees rather than inspire them. Leaders create visions to serve their own personal agendas and aim to create disciples rather than followers.

CULTURAL CONGRUENCE – WALK THE TALK

As a result of project work on organisational culture with our MBA students, it has become clear that one of the main causes of organisational culture veering towards the negative is a lack of congruence between what is being said and what is being done by those in leadership roles within their organisations. This failure to "walk the talk" leads to a lack of follower credibility in the organisation and in the top team. It sometimes requires tough decisions to maintain a congruence between espoused values and reality. However, the desired culture of the organisation needs to be seen to be reflected in the "acted upon" values of the CEO. Jack Welch of General Electric is one leader who is willing to "walk the talk". A firm believer in shared values, he maintains that the success of General Electric ... "depends on shared values ... the values-based organization ... derives its efficiency from consensus: workers who share their employer's goals don't need much supervision".[23]

In his restructuring efforts in GE he divided employees into four categories (see Figure 4.1 below). These divisions broke down into the following categories: those who possessed the right values and performed well (these were encouraged and rewarded); those who had the right values and performed poorly (these were trained and encouraged to develop skills); those who had the wrong values and performed poorly (let them go quietly); and finally those who had the wrong values and performed well. The treatment of this category demonstrates whether or not you walked the talk on the issue of organisational values. Jack Welch would advocate publicly getting rid of this type of employee if the values and culture of the organisation are to be credible. This latter category may appear to be beneficial to the organisation (high performance). However, the means by which they achieve this level of performance may be in opposition with the company's espoused values. This can create a huge dissonance amongst followers and can demotivate those with the right values.

STRATEGIC FOCUS AND COMPETING VALUES

The CEO does not work in a vacuum, but rather is positioned at the centre of many different competing constituencies. Each constituency will have both performance and behaviour expectations of the CEO, whose job is to balance the varied and sometimes conflicting demands placed upon him or her. The CEO will be required to choose between competing values including concern

Figure 4.1: Achieving Congruence between Organisational Values and Performance

HIGH PERFORMANCE

RIGHT VALUES		WRONG VALUES
Celebrate Reward Share		Sack Publicly
Develop skills Encourage Train		Let go quietly

LOW PERFORMANCE

for task versus concern for people, stability and efficiency versus flexibility and adaptation, and internal versus external focus. Each choice involves a trade off. Concern for task sometimes conflicts with the desires of organisational members. Should resources be allocated to members or invested into new technology? Should efficiency and economies of scale be the priority or should less structure and more flexibility?[24] It is the job of the senior team to achieve a balance between these competing values and the optimal balance will depend on the situational context and environmental challenges facing the business. Another balancing act that the CEO must perform is the management of internal and external constituencies.

Nadler and Heilpern identify two sets of external constituencies. One external group, comprising the financial community, suppliers and customers, is described as the "value chain constituency".[25] The other group, described as the social constituencies, includes the government and regulators, communities where the organisation operates and society at large.

Internal constituencies include: the board of Directors, as no other person in the organisation but the CEO has legitimate standing to deal with them; the TMG itself, because the CEO plays an important role in shaping, managing and driving this group; and finally the employees and enterprise at large are

Figure 4.2: The World of the CEO – 360 Degree Map

Adapted from Nadler D. A. and Heilpern, J. D. 1998. The CEO in the Context of Discontinuous Change. *Navigating Change: How CEOs, Top Teams and Boards Steer Transformation*, eds D. Hambrick, D. A. Nadler and M. L. Tushman. The Management of Innovation and Change Series. Harvard.

important, because in the CEO they see the single organisational leader. The CEO must negotiate a balance between these competing internal constituencies.

One of the most important activities of the senior group is to monitor the external environment; this provides the information needed for strategic planning and crisis management. While there is some debate as to how suitable long-term strategic planning is in a highly volatile and turbulent environment, it is necessary to be aware of the external constraints placed on the CEO in formulating strategy.

The amount of environmental scanning necessary will depend on how turbulent and dependent on outsiders (clients, suppliers, subcontractors and so on) the industry is. The more turbulent and externally dependent the industry is, the more environmental scanning needs to be undertaken. In order to do this, it is important to identify the relevant information and to use multiple sources of information to reduce biases. Sources of information include informal networks, publications, journals published by trade organisations and government reports. The sources used should be as objective and independent as possible.

CHANGE MANAGEMENT AND INNOVATION

Leading change is one of the most difficult leadership responsibilities. While it is beyond the scope of this chapter to fully address the area of change management, a discussion on leadership would not be complete without some reference to the role of the CEO as change agent.

In order to successfully introduce change, it is first necessary to understand the reasons why, for many, change is so threatening. Reasons for resistance to change include a lack of trust, belief that change is not necessary, belief that it is not feasible, loss of power and status, fear of personal failure and economic threats such as fear of downsizing and layoffs.[26]

Resistance to change is rarely a result of inflexibility or an inability to change; it is a very human and natural reaction which needs to be understood and accepted. Dissenters need to be engaged in open debate and won over by persuasion, not coercion.

In order to successfully guide change, it is necessary that there is a vision of a better future. Such a vision needs to be clear and achievable. The vision needs to contain strategic objectives which are tangible outcomes or results to be achieved. It is vital that organisational members are aware of the strategic importance of the change. Why are we engaging in change? Where does this change fit in with our strategy? Without this strategic focus, people may feel change is happening for change's sake.

It is imperative that key stakeholders are involved in the process. Key stakeholders might include owners, executives, customers, organisational members, investors and trade unions. Identify strategic objectives with wide appeal by involving all the stakeholders in the process and link these objectives to core competencies. It is vital that change is seen as achievable and within reach. A vision that is unrealistic and lacks credibility will ultimately fail.

Another important issue when implementing change is to understand the politics of change. The CEO needs to identify the key individuals whose support is crucial and build a broad coalition to support the change. It is also helpful to identify key dissenters and identify how to convert them whether it be through persuasion, rewards or coercion. Dissenters provide a valuable source of cognitive conflict and are a much easier persuasion target than the passive resister groups who nod acquiescence but engage in subterfuge to derail the change initiative. The CEO needs to be aware of the symbolic importance of a time of change, even the most banal activities can be given political significance. The CEO needs to be aware of the heightened interest in their activities and strive to achieve congruence between vision and action.

One effective method of introducing change is to provide organisational members with a rational plan. That does not mean the change process will take place according to this rational plan – change rarely does. However, the rational sell is a practical way of winning people over and is one of the most socially acceptable means of persuasion.[27] An effective technique demonstrated by Niall Saul during the turn around at Waterford Crystal is to involve everyone in this rational persuasion process. Present the facts to employees and ask them for their input. Ask them what they would do if they were running the business. The importance of understanding the political dimension of organisational change is explored in more detail in Chapter 6.

John Hunt at London Business School has outlined five ingredients necessary for successful change: pressure for change, direction and power, people's capacity to learn, actionable first steps and relevant rewards.[28] He maintains that each of these is equally important when driving for change. Without momentum or a need for change, organisations will be reluctant to fully engage in change. To bring about real change, there needs to be some external tension facing the company, for example, a hostile take over or a hostile major competitor. A leader can directly challenge the status quo by creating a sense of urgency. Tom Kasten, Vice President of Levi Strauss, used this approach:

> You create a compelling picture of the risks of not changing. We let our people hear directly from customers. We videotaped interviews with customers and played excerpts. One big customer said "We trust many of your competitors implicitly. We sample their deliveries. We open all Levi's deliveries". Another said "Your lead times are the worst. If you weren't Levi's, you'd be gone". It was powerful. I wish we had done more of it.[29]

Such techniques drive home in a very real way the need for change. For change to be successful, pressure for change is not enough. The change has to have drive and power behind it. All change involves power and the initiation of change must be driven from the top of the organisation. It is necessary that the people behind the change have the requisite power bases (authority, expertise, charisma, networks) to introduce change effectively. They also require the skills to promote an environment of learning to facilitate this change. This means sharing information and ideas, and enabling creativity and innovation.

In today's increasingly dynamic environment, providing support for innovation is a crucial aspect of leading the top team. However, research conducted by Michael West and colleagues indicates that this support is missing in many senior teams. Alarmingly, the teams studied scored lowest on the measure of support for innovation. It may be that the people who make up these teams are by nature critical and conservative in their orientations. Intelligent people usually do bring incisive critical orientations to problems and proposals. The problem with an overly critical approach is that many young, tender ideas are never nurtured to the stage of implementation because they are cut down while still weak. The history of science and of the study of successful R & D teams suggests that the most effective research teams are those which confirm early and disconfirm later. In successful teams, members tend to look for confirmation and support for each other's ideas in the early stages of the process and to bring a more critical disconfirming approach to the innovation proposal much later. A well-known motto at 3M is "It's better to ask forgiveness than to request permission."[30]

The next issue addressed by John Hunt is the provision of actionable steps. Have people the capacity and the power necessary to take the first steps? It is necessary that the skills, competencies and resources needed to take those first steps are available. If members feel real action is not an achievable goal, they will quickly become disheartened.

Finally, the power to bring about change depends on the rewards offered for change. If the organisational members benefit from change, they are much more likely to commit to it. The more the rewards for change are relevant to those involved, the more motivated they will be to make the journey.

DEFENCE MECHANISMS AND THE CEO

Throughout this chapter, we discussed how individuals hold theories or cognitive frames of reference that govern their actions and how such theories may inadvertently create organisational defensive routines that stifle innovation and learning. Argyris has identified two theories of action: the first he refers to as espoused theory which comprises beliefs, attitudes and values voiced by the individual; the second, theory-in-use, is the theory actually employed by the individual.[31] While one would expect there to be little difference between espoused theory and theory in use, the opposite has been found to be true.

There are frequently fundamental, systematic "mismatches" between people's espoused theory and theory in use, leading to the creation of defensive mechanisms in organisations which can block progress. Managers are very often unaware of this discrepancy. Also, this mismatch frequently happens when issues are threatening or embarrassing, the precise time when defensive routines may be detrimental.

Argyris defines defensive routines as "any action or policy designed to avoid surprise, embarrassment, or threat … prevent(ing) organisations from investigating or eliminating underlying problems".[32] The explanation for this, he maintains, lies in what he refers to as "skilled incompetence", where managers use practised routine behaviour (skill) to produce what they do not intend (incompetence). How can skilful behaviour be counter-productive? Managers are often skilful communicators. In order to avoid confrontation, they may not say what they really mean or test the assumptions they hold. However, this does not go unnoticed, but it does go undiscussed. The receiver of the communication may be aware that the message is incomplete, ambiguous or misleading and become suspicious. However, most likely they will not openly question the statement. Therefore, what is communicated verbally between individuals may not reflect each individual's inner dialogue. It requires confidence and courage to say "I don't quite understand what you're saying" or "I'm feeling a little uncomfortable with this issue". Instead, people say what they think other people want to hear and in doing so, paradoxically, create suspicion. Because neither party are willing to openly address the real issues at stake, this counterproductive communication continues.

Argyris claims the answer to this problem is learning. Individuals need to openly illustrate how they reached their evaluations, and inquiry and testing of these assumptions by others needs to be encouraged. Mike Fiszer in IMI echoed this need for openness and a certain amount of self-disclosure when discussing how to become a more effective leader. As a result, defensive routines are reduced, embarrassment and threat are not covered up but rather openly engaged.

This is by no means easy and is a lifelong process. It requires self-awareness and the ability to reflect. While many of the books and courses on management and leadership can be useful in motivating us towards this process, they by no means provide simple answers. That lies within the individual him/her self.

CONCLUSION

This chapter has looked predominantly at transformational leadership as the leadership style most suited to the 21st century team. We explored the importance of certain personal attributes of the leader including self-awareness and emotional intelligence in fostering an environment of trust, openness and innovation. Leaders create the context within which the members of the organisation operate and must continuously reflect upon both their own leadership style as well as its appropriateness to the demands placed upon the organisation which they lead.

This means successfully managing the many different tensions facing the leader – the struggle between stability and change, people and task, long term and short term, trust and uncertainty, consensus and conflict, and leading and serving.

Chapter 5

Conflict and the Top Management Team

Where there is imperfection there must be change. And to produce change, unless it is imposed by tyranny, there must be a difference of opinion; there must be opposition; there must be pioneer thinking; there must be a freedom to criticise; there must be the unremitting conflict and testing of ideas.

Ed Murrow[1]

INTRODUCTION

A discussion on top management teams would be seriously incomplete if it did not address conflict and its consequences for the team. There is a plethora of literature on when team conflict should be curbed and when it should be stimulated, what type of conflict is advantageous and how much. This chapter aims to address these issues in the context of the top management team.

Conflict occurs at every level of the organisation: at an interpersonal, inter-group and intra-group level. It occurs when an individual or group feels negatively affected by another individual or group. Most people feel uncomfortable with conflict and consider it as something to be avoided or resolved as quickly as possible. It can lead to stress and anxiety, breakdown of relationships, misunderstandings and a deterioration of social climate. However, research on conflict and its effects on individual, group and organisational performance is increasingly focused on the positive effects of conflict. This research argues that team conflict can be beneficial – indeed in some cases downright necessary – for high quality results. Increasing research emphasis is placed on the type of conflict which occurs, whether it is of a cognitive (task oriented) or affective (emotional) nature, and its relationship with decision quality and performance. In this chapter we will explore which type of conflict is beneficial to team functioning and describe some techniques to reduce the negative effects which certain types of conflict have on decision making, decision quality and decision implementation.

In Chapter 2 we argued that the top management team is quite different to other lower level teams in the organisation. Top management teams typically face situations of high ambiguity, high uncertainty and high complexity. Such teams are composed of individuals who are frequently individualistic and ambitious and who, in many instances, are heads of their own functions and departments. Often they are influenced and pressured by their own function or constituency to favour certain strategic decisions over others. The succession tournament for the position of CEO often further reduces the tendency for functional department heads to work together. As CEOs are generally more influential than other members due to power inequalities within the team, power disparities will also engender lobbying behaviours on the part of senior managers. Disharmony, debate and conflict are natural in such situations.

However, while a certain type of conflict (task) is invaluable when making strategic decisions, so too is the commitment to implementing the same decision. In order to gain the commitment necessary to implement a decision, consensus is a prerequisite. Because of the complexity and ambiguity surrounding strategic decisions, they are often difficult to articulate in detail. Numerous complications can arise with the implementation of strategic decisions. More than simple agreement is needed when obstacles such as resistance to change from other levels occur. Commitment is required and the willingness of the management team to weather the storm through difficult and often fraught situations.

Herein lies the dilemma facing top management teams: task conflict is valuable to heighten creativity and the critical capabilities of the team but it is also critical that this conflict does not destroy team commitment to the decision. Both conflict and consensus are required in tandem in order to formulate high quality decisions and to ensure that such decisions are implemented. But is the fusion of conflict and consensus a contradiction in terms? Research has shown that conflict and consensus need not be mutually exclusive. However, the relationship between the two depends on the type of conflict experienced. Different types of conflict have very different consequences for the satisfaction levels and performance of the team. The positive and the negative aspects of conflict are, however, sometimes very closely intertwined. Many studies indicate that cognitive (task) conflict can indeed be beneficial to team performance, reducing complacency and increasing creativity. However, while cognitive conflict has been found to enhance the quality of strategic decision making, interpersonal (affective) conflict can erode these benefits. Interpersonal conflict can have devastating effects on decision implementation. This highlights the importance of examining not just how much conflict exists within the team but, more importantly, whether it is of a task or emotionally laden nature.

SOME NEGATIVE CONSEQUENCES OF AVOIDING CONFLICT

The natural tendency, when dealing with conflict, is one of avoidance or suppression. We are programmed from an early age to avoid confrontation. Therefore, issues of contention may often be underplayed or denied. Research in group decision making has shown that the tendency of the leader is to suppress any potential conflict through strong demands for consensus. However, this attitude towards conflict in top teams is changing and some leaders are moving from conflict suppression to conflict management and, in certain cases, conflict stimulation.

That conflict suppression can have disastrous consequences is becoming more and more evident within top management teams. One of the most cited consequences is that of Janis's group-think phenomenon. This is one of the top five problems encountered by top management teams, according to Hambrick.[2] His research has uncovered a very real fear for CEOs – excessive like-mindedness and over cohesiveness at the top which Janis defines as group-think. In teams where group-think is prevalent, there is an absence of debate or genuine discussion. Such teams are usually defined by excessive cohesion and a lack of any critical evaluation of ideas. Team members are like minded and the tendency is to adopt strategies because they worked before rather than to explore alternative and potentially better strategies. Such a problem can even be difficult to identify simply because the team appears so harmonious and cohesive. It is often only after the implementation of a sub-optimal decision that the group-think problem can be recognised and diagnosed. Interestingly, it is often teams that are characterised by success that fall prey to this. Success can breed complacency which can lead to the demise of critical evaluation. Katz found that group tenure was linked to conflict norms and group-think.[3] Long tenured teams were found to lack internal tension, be extremely cohesive and sometimes "run on automatic pilot". Such teams need to introduce methods to counteract this.

CEOs in Hambrick's study expressed fears concerning lack of creativity, genuine debate and the prevalence of complacency in their management teams. A major problem facing such teams is how to devise a way to shake themselves out of complacency yet avoid the negative consequences of some of the processes used to do so. This fear was echoed by many of the CEOs participating in our study of top management teams in software and telecoms companies. There is a growing awareness that a lack of conflict within the team can be detrimental. The challenge lies in the ability to stimulate the right type of conflict. One software CEO is bringing in a consultant to work through the teams attitudes to conflict. She feels it has taken a long time to convey the message that questioning certain decisions is rewarded and that yes men are not what she is looking for. Her perseverance in introducing different attitudes to conflict is paying off and she feels her team is now more dynamic than ever.

> Conflict is something we encourage here – but in order to encourage the right kind – and for it to be of value – your team need to trust you. Without trust, all you will get are "yes men".
>
> CEO, software company

However, to be successful it is necessary for the leader to be personally able to take constructive criticism and to reward critical examination within the team. This can be difficult to achieve, as the top management team is different to many teams in another important way: the succession tournament. If the members of the senior team are competing for the coveted role of CEO this can hamper the decision-making climate within the top team leading to a stifling reduction in the cognitive conflict necessary for decision quality. If the incumbent CEO is influential in choosing his or her successor, team members may be reluctant to enter into open debate as they are competing with each other for the positive regard of the CEO.

Literature on emotional intelligence has highlighted the importance of self-confidence when dealing with conflict – individuals with high levels of self-confidence in their abilities were found to be more open to constructive criticism and less likely to take it personally. Because they were confident of their capabilities, being questioned or criticised did not put them on the defensive and the discussion that ensued was welcomed and regarded as beneficial.

The area of emotional intelligence in the workplace, particularly as one proceeds up the organisational hierarchy, is fast becoming recognised as an important key in resolving many of the dilemmas surrounding the area of conflict. One of the most pressing questions for many people dealing with conflict is how to stimulate positive conflict without opening the door to another type of dysfunctional conflict. Such a balancing act can be extremely difficult, as what starts out as cognitive or task-related conflict can so often deteriorate into emotional conflict. That does not imply that it is not possible. Indeed many top teams successfully tread this tightrope every day.

WHAT MAKES CONFLICT CONSTRUCTIVE?

Whether conflict is advantageous or not depends on the type of conflict, the situation surrounding the conflict and the outcomes desired.[4]

DIFFERENT TYPES OF CONFLICT

The type of conflict that exists within the team is directly related to the success of the team. Two different types of conflict have been identified: the first (cognitive or task conflict) has been found to yield positive results for the team; the second (affective or interpersonal conflict) has been found to have a negative impact on team performance.[5]

Figure 5.1: Two Different Types of Conflict and their Origins

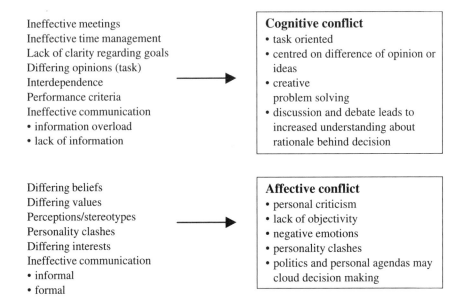

Ineffective meetings
Ineffective time management
Lack of clarity regarding goals
Differing opinions (task)
Interdependence
Performance criteria
Ineffective communication
• information overload
• lack of information

Cognitive conflict
• task oriented
• centred on difference of opinion or ideas
• creative
  problem solving
• discussion and debate leads to increased understanding about rationale behind decision

Differing beliefs
Differing values
Perceptions/stereotypes
Personality clashes
Differing interests
Ineffective communication
• informal
• formal

Affective conflict
• personal criticism
• lack of objectivity
• negative emotions
• personality clashes
• politics and personal agendas may cloud decision making

Cognitive conflict

> I don't think you are looking for people to just "get on with people", or people who are good with people … but I think that it is about working well together in a way that individuals can still retain their sharp edge and where we can still challenge each other and resolve differences …
>
> CEO interview, software company[6]

Cognitive conflict is task centred and arises from a difference in judgement or ideas about how best to carry out the task. This could relate to differing views or interpretations of future strategies or the establishment of goals. Cognitive conflict is unavoidable during strategic decision making or any non-routine decision-making situation. This arises as individuals are likely to perceive ambiguous or unclear situations in different ways and to make differing assessments about what the future may bring and, therefore, prefer different alternatives. This diversity of viewpoints can be very valuable to the organisation provided it is managed correctly. While cognitive conflict is defined as task centered, to say it is wholly without emotion would be inaccurate. Cognitive conflict may still cause stress and tension and can quickly disintegrate into affective conflict, especially if perceived as a personal attack or motivated by a political agenda. However, if cognitive conflict is dealt with in an impersonal manner, it has been found to intensify relationships and increase satisfaction. Trust within the group has also been found to moderate the relationship between task conflict and affective conflict.[7] Where trust levels are high within the top team, cognitive conflict is less likely to escalate into emotional conflict.

The techniques used to deal with cognitive conflict are very different to those necessary when the conflict is interpersonal in nature. Certainly, there is a confrontation of perspectives involved to resolve both types of conflict. This requires specifying the issue at hand and facilitating confrontation of both perspectives. This process may be very repetitive and an impasse can occur which compels parties to engage in further specification and confrontation. The means used when the conflict is task focused would include problem solving, debate and decision-making techniques. The open discussions and debate that occur increase understanding of the rationale behind decisions. Members feel involved in the decision-making process and, therefore, more committed to the decision itself. Debates thus become viewed as symbolic of fairness in the decision-making arena.

Task/cognitive conflict questionnaire

The following questionnaire explores the team's relationship with cognitive/task conflict. Team members fill out the questionnaire individually and then discuss their answers with the group. Does cognitive conflict occur within the team? Is constructive criticism encouraged? Do individual members adopt dissenting roles to ensure there is sufficient debate around issues? If the results from the questionnaire reflect an absence of debate of task-related issues, this might be an indication of over cohesiveness within the group and ways of stimulating cognitive/task conflict should be looked into.

Table 5.1: Cognitive/Task Conflict Questionnaire

1 = strongly agree; 2 = strongly disagree; 3 = neutral; 4 = agree; 5 = strongly agree
— Differences about the factual content of decisions rarely occur in this TMT
— There are many different ideas expressed in this TMT when making important decisions
— Decisions are openly discussed and critically evaluated within this team
— Constructive criticism is encouraged in this team
— We rarely disagree with each other about the strategic direction of the company
— If I question another member's idea, it can get personal
— When making decisions, at least one team member will assume the role of devil's advocate

Techniques to encourage cognitive conflict

Cognitive conflict is a prerequisite when making complex strategic decisions and can stimulate creative thinking. At Microsoft, for example, constructive dissent is facilitated and encouraged throughout the organisation. Bill Gates encourages dissenters to openly question a superior's perspective without fear of retribution. Motorola is another example of a company that stimulates a certain type of conflict. Motorola's practice of filing a "minority report" is where an employee is encouraged to go above their immediate supervisor and put forward a different point of view on a business decision. This practice has lead to many new and creative initiatives.[8]

The encouragement of cognitive conflict can take the form of very simple initiatives. One effective and relatively simple practice is that of negative brainstorming. Negative brainstorming is a particularly useful technique for promoting excellence and critical thinking in groups. It can be used for testing a new proposal or for evaluating an existing strategy, practice or objective. The technique can be achieved in the following three steps:

Step 1: once a promising idea has been proposed (or in the case of an existing practice, the practice or strategy has been clearly identified), the group brainstorms around all possible negative aspects or consequences of the idea. This brainstorming should be as uninhibited as positive. The intention is to generate a list of all the possible negative aspects of the idea or strategy no matter how wild or fanciful these possibilities might appear.

Step 2: team members choose four or five of the most salient criticisms and examine these in more detail. At least one of these criticisms should be a wild or fanciful criticism.

Step 3: the group then considers how the idea or existing practice could be modified to deal with each of the criticisms in turn. This third stage of the process is, therefore, essentially constructive in that the group is seeking to build on a new or existing practice in order to counter the major criticisms of it.

It may be that some fundamental weakness or difficulty is identified which the group sees no way of overcoming. In this case, the idea or the existing practice may be abandoned. However, this is a benefit rather than a disadvantage of the process since it enables groups to identify, at an early stage, any idea or approach which is likely to be unsuccessful.

This exercise is useful when an idea has reached the adoption and implementation phase of decision making. In addition to drawing out the weak points of an idea before it is implemented, it also encourages constructive criticism. People are sometimes inhibited in their criticisms for fear of causing offence. This approach makes it clear that criticism is directed at ideas and practices rather than people. If it is used on a regular basis "criticising ideas as a way of improving on them" becomes accepted by the group as good practice.

Another technique is to appoint a devil's advocate (DA). Their role is to offer dissenting voices and challenge the accepted way of thinking. This role can rotate and it is particularly effective at enabling junior members of the top team who may lack the confidence to present their own critique, but feel comfortable with offering objections and alternatives under the guise of DA. This role need not be occupied by one solitary individual. In fact it is probably better if a sub-group is appointed to this function. This sub-group should, however, remain sensitive to unpopular views and put forward alternative plans and options. Another strand of devil's advocacy is that of multiple advocacy (MA). Whereas basic DA is restricted to a single critique, MA results in many different critiques. This may involve many individuals playing the role of DA, representing multiple perspectives. It is important that the action of appointing a devil's advocate does not become counterproductive. Devil's advocacy can sometimes lead to a false sense of security with team members thinking "we have appointed a DA, therefore, we must be dealing with conflict" without actually fully engaging in the whole process. In such instances, DA becomes a false reassurance.

Another tactic suggested by Eisenhardt et al is the cultivation of a variety of distinct roles within the team.[9] Each role should represent a different approach to decision making and reflect the "fundamental tensions of managing in competitive high-velocity industries – i.e. short vs. long run, status quo vs. change, structure vs. flexibility". Team roles are discussed in more detail, in particular Belbin's team role theory in Chapter 2.

It is very possible that what starts off as task conflict can quickly transform into affective conflict, especially if the individuals involved are lacking in self-confidence and become defensive. Many of the positive features of task conflict, for example debate, multiple perspectives, confrontation, also have negative effects including dissatisfaction and frustration leading to interpersonal conflict. If ideas are rejected or questioned, team members may take it personally and begin to dislike other members. It is difficult to receive criticism in an objective manner and constructive criticism might be perceived as a personal attack. Politics, distrust and personal agendas can cloud decision making and valuable ideas may be discarded because of who proposed them. Such personal attributions might not always be voiced but they might fester and manifest themselves in other damaging ways.

Affective conflict

Affective conflict exists when disagreement is centered on non-work related issues. Jehn defines it as "where personal and relationship components within the group are characterised by friction, frustration and personality clashes within the group".[10] In a group where affective conflict was rife, there would be frustration, secrecy and a lack of trust. Group members tend to focus their efforts on solving or avoiding interpersonal conflicts rather than concentrating on task completion.

Affective conflict is particularly rife under conditions of change, especially under conditions of high growth. Under such circumstances, uncertainty is pervasive and many questions without clear-cut answers arise. This can have the effect of increasing political behaviour within the team and the encouragement of cliques. Suddenly every gesture takes on a symbolic significance and, very quickly, conflict begins to take its emotional toll.

Emotions are an important dimension of conflict. Karen Jehn defines the dimension of emotionality as the amount of negative affect felt during the conflict. Emotions reported during episodes of conflict include anger, rage, annoyance, frustration, uneasiness and discomfort. Jehn found that emotional conflict had a negative impact on team performance and satisfaction ratings, regardless of the types of conflict involved. It is, therefore, imperative to explore the role of emotion in intra-group conflict, particularly in the decision making of non-routine task groups.

The role emotions play in conflictual situations and the importance of emotional intelligence in resolving such situations have become widely recognised. Emotional intelligence should not be confused with being nice. Neither does it mean acting on our emotions. It does, however, mean managing our feelings and emotions so that they are expressed appropriately and effectively. In times of conflict, emotions sometimes come to the fore in ways that are not appropriate and may prevent people working towards their goals. It is especially important, under such tense and stressful situations, that the individuals involved are aware of a potential emotional explosion and take steps to avoid this. We have reviewed the five components of emotional intelligence in the last chapter when discussing leadership. The qualities of self-awareness, self-regulation and empathy are just as important in dealing with conflict.

Affective/interpersonal conflict questionnaire

This questionnaire examines the relationship between the top team and affective/interpersonal conflict. As before, the questionnaire is first completed individually. This is followed by a team discussion. This can be an effective way of dealing with previously unsurfaced issues that may hinder effective decision making, for example tension within the team. If the outcome of the team discussion is the realisation that high levels of affective conflict exist within the team, this can have disastrous effects on team performance and this needs to be addressed.

Table 5.2: Affective/Interpersonal Conflict Questionnaire

1 = strongly agree; 2 = strongly disagree; 3 = neutral; 4 = agree; 5 = strongly agree
— The members of the team get on well together
— Members of the TMT are willing to help each other out
— A win-lose attitude prevails within the top team
— There is tension between members of this team
— There is a great deal of competition between top team members
— There are personality clashes within this TMT
— There is a lack of trust within this team
— People look out for each other here

Have the whole team discuss team scores on this questionnaire and discuss whether there is a need to improve any of the above mentioned areas. Such tools are invaluable for the rich discussions that open up and promote a climate of open debate and questioning. It is necessary that the issues that arise are taken on board and that all involved feel the process is constructive and non-threatening.

PROBLEMS PREVENTING TMT SUCCESS

Of the five top problems faced by CEOs in managing the top team as identified by Hambrick, four are closely linked to affective conflict. Hambrick's research uncovered the following problems as being the most prevalent deterrents to successful team functioning:

• inadequate capabilities of an individual executive

• a common shortcoming of several or all team members

• harmful internal rivalries

• group-think

• team fragmentation.

Many of these problems can result in the transformation of cognitive conflict into affective conflict. Consider the first example in the list above, the shortcoming of a single executive. In the vast majority of cases, this was found to be related to task style or interpersonal skills rather than professional knowledge or skills. The problems found were short-sightedness when making strategic decisions, a lack of interpersonal and collaborative skills, and extreme ambition and politicisation. This can have a very negative effect on the top team itself and also tends to filter through to middle management. An abrasive personality can have negative effects for those who are responsible for implementing the strategic decisions. Abrasive individuals in the top team have been reported as undermining middle management's credibility by inappropriate outbursts and also providing harmful role models for other organisational members. Often, this behaviour is accepted because such individuals might get results. However, CEOs are becoming more and more aware of the short-sightedness of such behaviour. Jack Welch's philosophy is echoed here. High performers are inadequate if their values do not coincide with those of the organisation. People who get the right results through the wrong methods are not on the company's side in his view and their short-term positive results are far outweighed by the negative and far-reaching repercussions of their behaviour.

Just under a quarter of the CEOs in Hambrick's study identified harmful internal rivalries as a major problem. These rivalries were invariably between two team members rather than widespread political behaviour within the team. The consequence of harmful internal rivalries is a good example of the interplay between cognitive and affective conflict. It was found that the conflicts would start on relatively task-centered issues. However, what would begin as legitimate and cognitive conflicts tended to quickly deteriorate into affective conflict, focusing on issues of style and personality. CEOs reported having problems tackling the situation once it had entered into the mode of personal attacks. Even when tensions appeared to have subsided, an underlying ill will remained. Such divisions can have very detrimental effects on team functioning and effectiveness. However, some participants in our research study on software companies did not express surprise that such internal rivalries should exist.

> One of the hardest things in this job is trying to manage people – invariably egos will get in the way. How to deal with egos is one of the first lessons a CEO should learn as egos can cause simple conflicts to become very messy.
>
> CEO, software company

It is very easy for conflict of this type to disintegrate into petty squabbles characterised by a highly repetitive exchange of "Yes, you did" "No, I didn't" that goes in circles. Tact and diplomacy are invaluable when dealing with clashing egos – as is firmness. Sometimes a third party is necessary to stop worthless squabbling of conflicting egos. Because affective conflict requires very different handling techniques to cognitive conflict (the more rational techniques of debate, problem solving and effective meeting techniques would not be suitable here), it is sometimes necessary for an impartial outsider to help the process on. Affective conflict requires empathy and understanding and this can require training in the expression of feelings and frustrations, the development of mutual acceptance and openness, and the establishment of trust.

The importance of empathy and trust was explored in Chapter 4 on leadership. These attributes are especially important when dealing with affective conflict which is concerned with emotions rather than task-focused issues. It is necessary that these attributes are valued by the leader and are seen to be in place (again, if the leader does not "walk the talk" there will be scepticism and mistrust). In order to establish these values within the group, time, reflexivity (team reflection) and a certain positive motivation from all members of the team is vital.

On occasion, relations between two team members are at an impasse and a third party may be required to step in. This could be another team member but often, because complete objectivity is needed, it is best to use a consultant. The consultant would meet with the two parties and discuss how each feels about restoring cooperation. They will each take turns in talking about any behaviour of the other that frustrates them. Throughout the process, the consultant will check whether each party's message is clear to the other. Often such rivalries are borne out of petty misunderstandings early on and this process can help clarify intentions.

However, re-establishing goodwill among team members is not always so simple; sometimes an understanding of the other point of view is not the outcome. The solution may be to accept differences and tolerate a certain amount of tension within the team.

The time spent discussing the issue and the resulting increase in understanding usually benefits the situation, as one of the chief executives in our study of software companies pointed out:

> If I encounter tension or antagonism within the team, I insist on openness. We go out and thrash out the issue over a few pints. Most of the time, this really seems to work.

THE NEW APPROACH TO CONFLICT

As discussed above, the type of conflict that exists within the team will determine whether the outcome will be positive or negative. This growing awareness that a certain type of conflict is necessary and ought to be encouraged was voiced by nearly all our respondents. Certainly, the norm for increased openness within the team was one adopted by many of the CEOs participating in our study. When asked how tensions were dealt with within the team, the vast majority opted for open frank discussion.

The research by Jehn also supports this approach.[11] Openness towards the expression of conflict was found in many cases to be beneficial to team functioning, especially when the conflict was task oriented. However, conflict norms become more problematic when dealing with affective conflict. There is conflicting evidence to suggest that the openness norm can be beneficial here. While Jehn found many successful teams displayed a norm of openness when dealing with task conflict, the opposite was the case when the conflict was affective. In the teams which she researched, open discussion surrounding interpersonal problems was not encouraged. However, there is some research that suggests that teams which are openly able to discuss socioemotional issues are much more cohesive. The underlying issue here may be how prepared these teams are to deal with the repercussions of such discussions. Certain procedures and skills need to be in place and the team may require training in communication skills, listening skills and the ability to empathise. This requires trust, motivation and commitment from the CEO and all the members of the team, both in terms of time and personal input.

REFLEXIVITY

Self-reflection and reflexivity within the team increase team members' comfort around uncertainty and conflict. Teams where members are committed to being effective in their work are more likely to reflect upon the appropriateness of their process, task outcomes and strategies, and modify them accordingly. Reflection consists of attention, awareness and monitoring, and evaluation of the object of reflection. It includes behaviours such as questioning, planning and divisive exploration. As reflection takes time and effort, it is necessary that the CEO is behind the process and that all the team members support it. It is also necessary that there is frequent interaction among team members. This enables members to clarify their own and other team members' position on different issues. It also means members will become more comfortable with each other and less constrained by politeness to the rest of the team.

THE TMT AND CONFLICT OUTSIDE THE TEAM

Interestingly, a dilemma voiced by a considerable number of the CEOs in our software survey concerned dealing with conflict outside the TMT. All of the companies interviewed were operating in high tech, non-routine environments employing highly professional knowledge workers. Such workers are entering the organisation with very different expectations and they are very aware that demand for their skills far exceeds supply. This, many respondents feel, has created the need to develop very unique corporate cultures. Managing such a high power, knowledge-based workforce is taking a substantial amount of the CEO's time. There are certain factors that differentiate this industry from others. Many of the companies are relatively new (under five years) and relatively small (under 100 employees). Employees are highly qualified and experts in the area; most of the work is centred around teams and is project based. This requires finely tuned management skills such as rotating project leaders and building cross-functional teams which can cause tension to arise between employees. One CEO interviewed felt that 80 per cent of his time was taken up with dealing with interpersonal issues associated with such schemes. Many of these software companies, while relatively small, are recognising the need for a specific human resource specialist to advise on these issues.

SELF-AWARENESS AND CONFLICT MANAGEMENT SKILLS

Every individual has his or her own unique conflict handling style. How one feels about confrontation and conflict depends very much on the personal attributes of the individual and his or her past experience of conflict. In order to successfully manage conflict, it is necessary to become aware of your own underlying assumptions about it. Instruments such as the Thomas-Kilmann Conflict Mode Instrument examine the respondents' preferred strategies when dealing with conflict. Such instruments are useful in heightening our awareness of preferred or dominant strategies and how inappropriate/appropriate these may be, depending on the situation.

Thomas and Kilmann describe a person's behaviour in conflict situations along two basic dimensions – assertiveness and cooperativeness. These can be used to define five main conflict-handling strategies in their instrument (see diagram overleaf).

We usually have a personal preference for a certain strategy when dealing with conflict. However, this can create problems if we over-rely on that strategy, employing it in situations that may not be appropriate. The Thomas-Kilmann instrument is useful in that it heightens our awareness of our dominant, preferred strategy and outlines situations where it may not be most effective. It also illustrates some pitfalls associated with each preference. For example, there may be a tendency for those with a preference for competing to be surrounded by yes men as people learn it may be unwise to disagree.

Those with a preference for collaboration may sometimes waste time discussing issues in depth that do not merit this level of attention. Collaborators need to distinguish between situations that require quick decisive action and the more important issues that require organisational support and commitment. If compromise is the dominant strategy, reliance on the practicalities and tactics of compromise may cause the individual to lose sight of larger issues. Individuals who respond to conflict through avoidance sometimes overlook issues, give input reluctantly and may be far too cautious. Those with a

Figure 5.2: Conflict Resolution Strategies

Competition Behaviour is assertive and uncooperative – attempts to overwhelm other party threats, use of power. Win-lose mentality.	**Collaboration** Behaviour is assertive and cooperative, joint problem solving with other party to find solution that benefits both. Win-win mentality.
Avoidance Unassertive and uncooperative. Withdrawal from or suppression of signs of conflict, while not actually cooperating with other party. Win-lose mentality.	**Accommodation** Behaviour is assertive and cooperative, sacrifices own aim in the interest of other party. Win-lose mentality.
Compromise Intermediate amounts of assertive and cooperative. Behaviour in which the person forsakes some of own aims in return for satisfaction or others. No winners, no losers.	

preference for accommodation may feel their own ideas are not getting the attention deserved and may harbour feelings of frustration.[12]

While this is a very superficial glance at the effects of conflict management styles, it is worth taking into account the effects of your own particular style and when and where it is most appropriate

WHEN TO USE DIFFERENT CONFLICT MANAGEMENT TECHNIQUES

The following are a set of recommendations for conflict management developed by Thomas and Kilmann.

Use competition when:

• quick, decisive action is necessary

• the future popularity of decision is unimportant

• the matter is essential to organisational success

- one or both of the parties would take advantage of the other's less competitive behaviour.

Use avoidance when:

- the issue is trivial
- neither party has a chance of satisfying concerns
- people need time to cool down
- more information is needed to bring a resolution
- there are hidden agendas and the apparent issue could mask something more fundamental.

Use compromise when:

- the parties' goals are important but not worth the disruption that may arise from using more assertive approaches
- the parties have equal power and stalemate is likely
- temporary settlements are needed
- time is short.

Use accommodation when:

- one party is patently in the wrong
- the issue is much more important to one party than the other
- a trade off for an issue to be established later
- you wish to build social credits.

Use collaboration when:

- time is plentiful
- it is vital that both parties learn from the experience
- gaining commitment of both parties to implementation is vital
- it is necessary to work through feelings that may give rise to future conflict.

DIFFERENT CONFLICT SITUATIONS

While it appears evident that whether conflict is beneficial to group perform-ance depends very much on the type of conflict experienced, it has also been found to depend very much on the decision-making environment. In groups performing very routine tasks, both task and relationship conflict were found to be detrimental. This is not surprising. Routine tasks have low levels of variability and are characterised by high levels of certainty. Task conflict here, therefore, is a hindrance. In contrast, non-routine tasks involve high levels of variability. There is a high level of variety and the tasks are characterised by high levels of ambiguity and uncertainty. Research has shown that in contrast to routine task groups, non-routine task groups are not adversely affected by conflict. However, as mentioned earlier, this is highly dependent on the type of conflict involved and the level of conflict. At times, cognitive conflict has been found to be beneficial in non-routine decision-making groups. Because such groups have few set procedures and are engaged in problem solving under conditions of uncertainty, non-routine groups were found to benefit from the diverse ideas of other group members.[13] Task conflict was found to reduce complacency, increase critical evaluation and decrease the group-think phenomenon.

Routine and non-routine tasks are analogous with Mischel's strong and weak situations.[14] Strong situations are characterised by a high degree of certainty, clear guidelines, historical norms or generally accepted patterns of behaviour, including specific societal or organisational norms of emotional expression. Weak situations, however, are characterised by a much greater degree of uncertainty where no such clear guidelines exist. In strong situations personality may play a relatively small role as such situations lead people to construe events in similar ways, produce uniform expectations for role and emotional performance and incentive patterns, and provide the requisite skills. Weak situations, however, are not interpreted or construed in similar ways, do not provide uniform expectations about performance and incentives, and may not provide the requisite skills. In weak situations, individual differences such as personality can be expected to exert a greater influence on behaviour. Emotionality certainly matters here as resistance to change and associated feelings of fear, frustration, anxiety, shame and anger will trigger various defence mechanisms.[15] The senior team regularly faces non-routine, highly complex situations, therefore, cognitive conflict, if managed appropriately, can increase the creativity and innovation used in making difficult decisions. Because these situations may not be uniform and interpretations may be diverse, personality and emotional intelligence play major roles in how people react to questioning or open discussion. Helpful team processes may be in place, for example, negative brainstorming and team reflexivity, but without the presence of personal attributes such as self-confidence and self-control and without social skills such as empathy and negotiation, there will be a high risk that functional conflict will disintegrate into petty squabbling. Below are some reminders in order to keep affective conflict at bay.

Table 5.3: Checklist to Keep Conflict Functional

Keep conflict functional!
Use appropriate conflict handling technique
Be aware of conflict norms within the group
Reflexivity within the group
Establishment of devil's advocate or dialectic inquiry
Be aware of self-fulfilling prophecies
Be aware of perceptual biases
Communication quality
Be aware of the importance of emotion in conflict
What are the underlying concerns?
Is there trust in the group?
Be aware of competition for its own sake
How egocentric are the players?
What kind of games are people playing?

CONCLUSION

In this chapter, we discussed the recent change in organisational thinking concerning the usefulness of conflict in the top management team. However, whether conflict is positive or not for the team depends on the type of conflict encouraged. We discussed the difference between cognitive and affective conflict and how the former can lead to increased creativity and higher quality decisions and how the latter can lead to team dysfunction. We outlined some of the techniques available to stimulate cognitive conflict while negating affective conflict, including devil's advocacy and multiple advocacy. The skilled CEO/chairman needs to be constantly vigilant in the presence of conflict and harness its power, while mitigating its sometimes negative effects.

Chapter 6

Power and the Top Management Team

That all driving force is will to power, that there is no other physical, dynamic or psychic force except this.

Nietzsche[1]

INTRODUCTION

The senior management team is composed of individuals with a variety of backgrounds, experience, expertise and, usually, different levels and sources of power. The relative power of each member of the TMT must be taken into account when discussing issues such as composition, structure, leadership and team processes including communication and consensus building. While CEOs are generally more influential than others, there are circumstances when managers may hold power due to particular expertise, prestige by virtue of their ownership position, external connections or tenure, as stated by one CEO below:

> We have gone through an acquisition where we took over a company of our own size, and so we selected the on-going top management team from both existing teams ... therefore, some of the members of the TMT have only been within the new team for a short while (1 year) ... I would feel the power distribution within the group is influenced by the length of time in the group
>
> CEO, software company[2]

Depending on the decision to be made or the action to be taken, the theory suggests that levels of power fluctuate within the team at different times. If the emphasis is on selling, marketing may hold the reins, whereas if the strategic direction is towards cutting costs, the finance department may be at the fore. Different decisions or contingencies will require different types of expertise which may propel individual team members into positions of power at different times. Reliance on a single indicator of power, for example, position power, ignores the fact that power in this domain is multidimensional encompassing expert power, prestige power and charismatic power to name but a few sources of power. Different sources of uncertainty will require different individuals/groups/departments to cope, hence power is never static. However, in reality, situational factors might not affect the power distribution as significantly as the theory suggests. Ruairi O'Flynn at the Irish Management Institute (IMI) feels that the impact of situational factors might sometimes be exaggerated:

> I'm not convinced that levels of power fluctuate within teams due to changing priorities. My experience is that the force of individual characteristics regarding top team members is not changed by situational factors, unless there is a change in the make up of the team.

THEORIES OF POWER

In order to understand the complexity of power, theorists have tried to categorise the many different sources of power. One of the most conventional typologies is that of French and Raven who identify five major sources of power: reward power, coercive power, legitimate power, expert power and referent power (see diagram overleaf).[3] These sources of power are not mutually exclusive and are very often used in unison, for example the CEO will not rely solely on position power to lead the team; he or she may also lead by virtue of their expertise, contacts or reputation. However, Fergus Barry of the IMI feels that certain sources of power are still underused in practice:

> In covering "Power" as a topic in management development programmes I find that many managers have not analysed what power is, how personal power is developed and how best to use it. Analysis of feedback instruments used suggests that most managers build their power on the bases of expertise and position. What are often neglected are referent power (a manager with a clear and attractive picture of where he/she is going and how he/she expects the team to work together to achieve the vision) and connection power (networking). This suggests that managers need to concentrate more on developing their personal power in these areas.

A useful typology for senior management that expands on the French and Raven classification is that of Finkelstein.[4] He has identified four key power bases within the top management team: structural/hierarchical power, prestige power, ownership power and expert power as illustrated by Figure 6.2.

Figure 6.1: Integrating French and Raven and Finkelstein's Classification of the Sources of Power

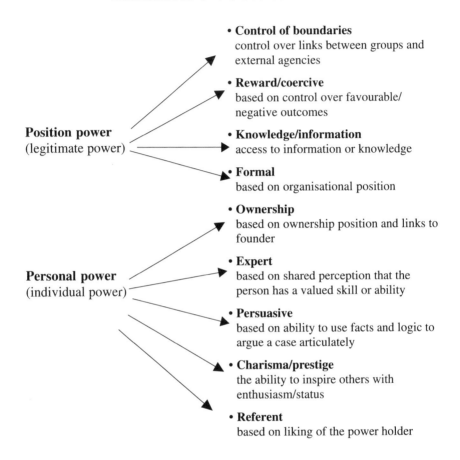

Position power
(legitimate power)

• **Control of boundaries**
control over links between groups and external agencies

• **Reward/coercive**
based on control over favourable/ negative outcomes

• **Knowledge/information**
access to information or knowledge

• **Formal**
based on organisational position

Personal power
(individual power)

• **Ownership**
based on ownership position and links to founder

• **Expert**
based on shared perception that the person has a valued skill or ability

• **Persuasive**
based on ability to use facts and logic to argue a case articulately

• **Charisma/prestige**
the ability to inspire others with enthusiasm/status

• **Referent**
based on liking of the power holder

Figure 6.2: Examples of Finkelstein's Key Power Bases of Top Management Team Members

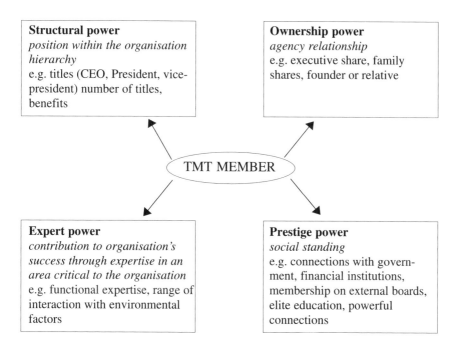

Structural power
position within the organisation hierarchy
e.g. titles (CEO, President, vice-president) number of titles, benefits

Ownership power
agency relationship
e.g. executive share, family shares, founder or relative

TMT MEMBER

Expert power
contribution to organisation's success through expertise in an area critical to the organisation
e.g. functional expertise, range of interaction with environmental factors

Prestige power
social standing
e.g. connections with government, financial institutions, membership on external boards, elite education, powerful connections

Adapted from Finkelstein, S. 1992. Power in Top Management Teams: Dimensions, Measurements and Validation. *Academy of Management Journal*, 35(3): 505-537.

Structural power

Structural power is synonymous with hierarchical power, formal power or position power. It is power accrued from the formal structure of the organisation and denotes the legislative right to exert influence. The CEO, because of his or her position in the hierarchy, possesses very high structural power.[5] Such authority enables CEOs to cope with uncertainty through the influence they have over the members of the dominant coalition. Structural power may vary amongst top managers (some may be more privy to certain information than others) and the greater this source of power, the more influential the position within the TMT. While the position of CEO denotes power in itself, holding multiple titles, for example being a member of the board of directors, is a further indicator of structural power. Finkelstein (1992) has highlighted that the CEO may also jointly serve as board chairperson, which enables him or her to control the agenda of board meetings, thus controlling information that the board receives.

Ownership power

Finkelstein defined ownership power as "the strength of a manager's position in the principal agent relationship".[6] This is related to the size of share holding a TMT member may have or their links to founders of the company. Individuals with high ownership power often wield considerable influence over the board of directors and can exert great influence over the firm's direction. Individuals who have increased interaction or strong relationships with the founders of the company or board members may also exert more influence over strategic decisions.

Expert power

Dealing with environmental contingencies is another key source of power. The task environment is often a very significant source of uncertainty within the organisation as customers, suppliers and competitors can all behave in unforeseen ways. The more contact and the better the relationship between the manager and these components of the external environment, the greater their expert power. This is especially the case if the expertise lies in an area critical to the particular organisation. A comprehensive knowledge of firm specific information can mean control over directors' access to such information.

Prestige power

The personal status of the top team member in society can also lead to the perception of power within the organisation. The position and reputation of the CEO in the external environment, for example, the government, financial institutions and other companies may be of value to the organisation. Membership of external boards, for example, may lead to information on business conditions that may not otherwise be available. Such connections may also hold symbolic importance. Jack Sparks of Whirlpool recognised the importance of good contacts:

> I wasn't in line to be the CEO … I kept outside contacts. I went to Conference Boards. I went to marketing seminars. I went … where I thought I could meet people and learn. As a consequence, I built up a wide acquaintance in not only the business world but also the academic world.[7]

CEOs may associate themselves with a member of government or other leaders in order to enhance their public image. Such relationships may serve to enhance the legitimacy of the CEO. However, there is the always danger that if the person the CEO has chosen to be symbolically linked with falls from grace, the reputation of the CEO may suffer also.

The resource-based theory of power

Power may also be examined through the lens of the resource-based theory. This perspective maintains that power is derived from control over such resources as people, money, time or knowledge. People possess different sources of power, depending on the particular resource at their disposal. Control over financial details may lead to reward or coercive power, charisma to referent power, information to expert power and contacts or status to prestige power. A single resource may lead to an increase in many different power bases. Information may lead to an increase in expert power, but it might also increase less obvious sources of power. As Ruairi O'Flynn at the IMI observes "I've seen information/network add to referent power: they knew he was well connected around the organisation and it added to his appeal, so referent power may not be just charisma."

While the control over resources leads to the dependency of others and, therefore, is the key to power, it is important that the resource you control is in demand. In other words, the resource should be deemed important, scarce and non-substitutable.[8] If the resource is perceived as unimportant, there will be no demand! The resource must also be scarce – the more plentiful the resource, the less power it holds. For many industries knowledge is a scarce resource, therefore, knowledge is power. This can often lead to a reluctance to share knowledge with others. Where certain information is vital, those who possess that information are in a position of power. The desire to retain such a powerful position may prevent access to such information, often obstructing organisational learning. Thus, an effective power tactic is to become the sole conduit of certain information. It is also necessary that the resource is non-substitutable; the resource must be unique and cannot be replaced by something else. Many industries, especially knowledge-based industries, realise that in a high-tech world the most non-substitutable resource is their people.

COPING WITH UNCERTAINTY

Power is inextricably linked with the perceived ability to cope with uncertainty. In order for an individual to hold power, they must be perceived as capable of managing/coping with uncertainty. Each of the different sources of power may be viewed as methods through which the CEO can manage uncertainty. For example, structural power can minimise uncertainty by controlling information disclosed to the board or by controlling the agenda in order to deal with dissidents (see Table 6.1). Expert power (especially relevant to the CEO's boundary spanning role) is essential in coping with uncertainty externally in the task environment. Functional expertise opens up opportunities to develop contacts both within and outside the firm, equipping the CEO to better address environmental uncertainties. Prestige power, in the form of membership of external boards, can lead to information that may not otherwise be available but which may be of value to the organisation

Table 6.1: Head of University – Power Tactics to Quell Dissent[9]

A UK University, acclaimed for research, faced an audit for teaching quality. A research assessment exercise was also imminent. The senior team was faced with three options:

Continue as before, concentrating on research and accept low teaching rating.

Focus on research while doing just enough to get a satisfactory rating on teaching.

Put all efforts behind teaching and aim for excellence. The head reached a decision quickly, realising that to fail on teaching would reflect poorly on the college and would provide ammunition to opponents. However, there was a minority within the senior team who felt all efforts should continue behind research. These individuals voiced their dissent publicly and the decision was losing credibility. One individual in particular was especially vocal in his opposition.

The solution adopted by the senior team was to engage in a series of effective spoiling tactics. Arranging premeetings without this individual, putting his issues last on the agenda so there would be no time to discuss it properly, enlisting the support of junior staff behind the venture and urging them to spread the word. They also resorted to a little innuendo, in order to damage his credibility. The head of the University justified this behaviour as inevitable:[10]

"I don't see how I could have acted differently in the circumstances, without accepting damage to my own reputation, as well as that of my school and perhaps the institution ... I don't regard any of this as unethical. On the contrary, to have ignored the issue, or to have just walked away from it, would have been difficult for me to defend. We got the 'excellent' rating."

NETWORK THEORY AND CENTRALITY

Yet another theory of power is based on the positive relationship found between power and influence and the centrality of one's position.[11] This might include centrality within the TMT, within the organisation, across organisations, professionally or politically. This theory is based on the interpersonal nature of power and holds that one can acquire power through the establishment of networks or relationships with significant others. This theory works along the premise that "you are who you know" and being connected in all the right places is viewed as critical.

How central an individual actually is within the organisation depends on how direct the links are between him or her and the web of contacts they possess. The more direct the connections, the less is the need for the individual to rely on others to mediate for access to certain resources. Centrality can also refer to the mediating positions a person may occupy. This refers to the intermediary positions a person may occupy in connecting other individuals. The more people rely on you to link them with others – be they external organisations, clients or the CEO – the more power you accrue.

This theory is linked to the power stratagem of building alliances, for example through appointments and promotions or through favours.[12] Lee Iacocca was only too aware of the importance of strong alliances. He understood that in order to turn around Chrysler, he needed the support of many constituencies. He spent a large degree of his time lobbying groups in Washington to get a loan from the government and networked with dealers and suppliers. He also made strategic placements on the Board of Directors.[13] A politically astute leader will make a point of building alliances with those above and below him or her. Alliances provide ready made systems of communication through which the leader can learn the reactions to decisions and what barriers may lie ahead. One form of alliance is the sponsor-protégé relationship. Such an alliance provides the protégé with channels for advancement and the sponsor with a group of loyal supporters.

A good example of this is the relationship between Frank Stanton and William Paley at CBS. Frank Stanton was known to possess high interpersonal skills and quickly learnt that to survive at CBS, he would have to manage his relationship with Paley carefully. Paley was volatile and was known to fire people without warning. While the two individuals were very different, a sponsor-protégé relationship developed between the two.

> Although Stanton was only seven years younger than Paley, the two men assumed a father-son relationship marked by Stanton's unwavering filial respect ... in the presence of their subordinates ... In meetings, Stanton submerged his ego, never taking issue with Paley.[14]

This worked well for both – Stanton had autonomy over operations while Paley retained ultimate authority. However, sometimes the sponsor-protégé relationship can move from being a mutually beneficial arrangement to becoming an arrangement that benefits only one, as in the CBS case:

> As Stanton grew more experienced, he learned to reflect an opposing viewpoint by attributing it to others ... When Stanton expressed his own opinion, it was to agree with the boss.

DIFFERENT TYPES OF TMT POWER DISTRIBUTION

The deployment of power will also depend on the type of top management team in existence. A study conducted by researchers at the University of Maryland and the University of Limerick provides a description of some of the different types of top management teams they encountered in Ireland and the US while conducting research on the effects of structure, composition, leadership and power on the TMT.[15] They came up with the following principal clusters which they describe as: hierarchy, blue chip, federation and headless group.

Figure 6.3: Power in Four Types of Top Management Team

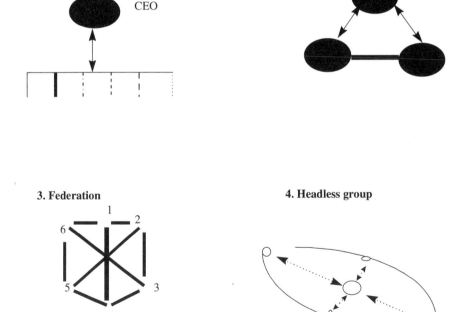

Adapted from Clark et al. 1997. Configuration of Top Management Teams: Structure, Composition, Process, Power and Leadership. Paper presented at the Organisational and Management Theory Division of the Academy of Management at the annual meeting in Boston.

Hierarchical TMT

The defining characteristics of the hierarchical team are low empowerment of the team combined with high levels of experience and heterogeneity. Teamwork and leadership are moderate in these teams and the CEO tends to be the key decision maker. The diversity within the team suggests a variety of different perspectives and the high level of experience would indicate that the information funnelled to the CEO would be of high quality. However, this high quality information was often not utilised.

This TMT cluster was found to be one of the lowest ranking in innovative measures as, despite being a heterogeneous team, the TMT members were disempowered. This unbalanced distribution of power resulted in a "lack of voice of team members … eliminated the opportunity to share unique visions of the competitive environment".[16] This reliance on hierarchical position limited the role of each TMT member to their particular functional area and constrained the free flow of information.

The blue chip

The defining characteristics here are extreme high empowerment and experience. It is also characterised by homogeneity and moderate levels of teamwork, leadership and formal communication. The high level of experience within the team may contribute to the high level of empowerment, however, the leader in this team appears also to be willing to share power.

Sharing of power and the resultant increase in TMT member voice can potentially lead to problems achieving discourse. However, this is not the case with the blue chip group, due to the high level of team composition homogeneity. While the decision-making process is quite smooth in this team, it is open to the risk of group-think. Unsurprisingly, this team was found to be very low on innovation and to rely heavily on existing markets. While team members were empowered, they were found to have very similar opinions and values as the leaders. This homogeneity may circumscribe their ability to test new waters. Another reason for this team's reliance on existing markets may be the high level of experience of the team. Familiarity with their markets may deter them from entering into uncharted territory.

Blue chip was found to be a high performing team. The experience of the team and the familiarity with the existing markets prove to be a potent combination. Due to the emphasis on established markets, team similarity does not seem to be a negative factor. The emphasis is on implementation, not innovation.

The federation

This cluster is characterised by a fairly even distribution of power within the TMT and high levels of teamwork but a complete lack of leadership. The composition of this team is heterogeneous with experience being low, and the use of formal channels of communication also being low. The researchers found that many of the teams they identified as federations were composed of inexperienced managers who they felt were perhaps "substituting empowerment and teamwork for leadership".[17] While the federation lacked a central figure or a key decision maker, it functioned – perhaps due to high levels of social integration within the group. It was also efficient because each TMT member exercised discretion over their own area of expertise. This power sharing was vital since no one individual had sufficient experience to make big decisions. The extreme heterogeneity provided variation in types of experience which seemed to supply a viable alternative to a central figure.

This cluster was found to be the most innovative. It was found to derive more revenue from new markets than established markets. It also had high levels of empowerment and the high levels of diversity led to open sharing of a wide variety of ideas about the environment, resulting in innovative solutions. This team was also associated with high performance organisations, which focus on new products aimed at new markets. The emphasis in this configuration is on innovation.

The headless group

The defining characteristics here were generally low levels of empowerment, experience, heterogeneity and communication. Lack of experience would suggest a need for guidance. However, there is also a lack of leadership. In this team, the CEO is often simply a figurehead.

Surprisingly, this team was found to be innovative. The researchers explain such a perplexing result by suggesting that, while selling new products in new markets may be a sign of forward thinking and innovation, it may also result from an inability to sustain growth in new product introductions and poor customer retention. The performance of the cluster would give an indication of which would be the truer story: the performance of this cluster was not high and was found only to be average for the sample.

The description of these clusters demonstrate the importance of looking at the TMT from a multitude of dimensions. Power is a very important and necessary factor to include in assessing the performance of each group as this research has shown.

USES AND MISUSES OF POWER IN TOP TEAMS

As stated earlier, to categorise power and politics in simplistic terms such as legitimate/illegitimate would be to oversimplify the reality of organisational life. Power and politics are part of everyday life. Power may be deployed for a variety of different reasons, sometimes in the interest of the organisation, sometimes in the interest of progression or personal gain. "Spoiling tactics" can include controlling the agenda, placing undesirable individuals or proposals at the end of the agenda (less time to discuss it and sometimes less people present), scheduling meetings without contacting certain individuals, targeting opinion leaders and deal making, and marginalising dissidents through innuendo in order to discredit them. These tactics can be employed in order to ostensibly protect the organisation (perhaps that senior dissident refuses to accept advantageous and necessary strategic change) or they may be engaged in for less laudable reasons.

Reasons for political behaviour depend on the type of individual involved, the personal motives and the organisational circumstances. Research has shown that certain individuals are more political than others. For example Machiavelians are more likely to exercise subtle control over others, are adept at manipulating them and are more disposed to use politics. People with authoritarian personalities often like high risk situations and are more likely to engage in the use of politics.[18] McClelland and Atkinson's work studying the motivational bases of human nature identifies three main individual motives: the need for achievement, the need for affiliation and the need for power.[19] In studying the nature of these needs, McClelland and his colleagues proposed a personality profile labelled the Leadership Motive Profile which related to effective leadership.[20] According to McClelland, the effective leader is likely to have a high need for power (self-direction, concern for prestige, high energy), a lower need for affiliation (need for close relationships) and, under certain circumstances, a low need for achievement (need for personal accomplishment). The effective leader was also more likely to use power to achieve institutional goals rather than personal goals.

This need for power can be linked to House's theory of charismatic leadership.[21] He identifies charismatic leaders as having a high need for influence or power. Without such a need, he maintains, these leaders are unlikely to have developed such persuasive skills to influence others and they are also likely to obtain satisfaction from the leadership role. The need for power and the intensity of this need is viewed by some as the outcome of a gradual developmental process, dependent on the individual's relationship with the environment. Karen Horney identifies two different needs for power: a normal need for power and a neurotic need for power.[22] While the normal striving for power is based on the realisation of our strengths and capabilities, the neurotic need for power is based on feelings of insecurity, anxiety and helplessness and can often be traced back to childhood experiences. Studies linking the need for power and power styles with childhood experiences of authority and control, parental styles, relationships with siblings and background have been conducted by writers such as Manfred Kets de Vries[23] and Amy Stark.[24] Looking at power orientation as a developmental process, Manfred Kets de Vries identifies three different power styles: the persuasive style, closely linked to charismatic leadership; the coercive style, linked to the leaders position and ability to influence through control; and the manipulative style, which has close connections with Machiavellian power tactics.[25]

However, political behaviour cannot simply be ascribed to personality factors. Organisational factors come into play also. Ambiguity about goals or roles within the organisation can lead to higher instances of politicking. Vagueness can be used to justify almost any course of action that could be used for personal gain by saying that it will help achieve the goal. Scarce resources introduce competition and the inevitability of there being winners and losers. Tactics such as lobbying or presenting misleading information may be resorted to in order to secure certain resources. Unclear criteria for evaluating performance often rely on subjective evaluation guidelines. Again this can lead to increased politicking as individuals attempt to redefine their role in an advantageous way. Politics are inextricably linked with organisational life and political acumen is a necessity in understanding why certain things are done, what is being said and the symbolic importance of certain gestures. Research has shown that individuals high in empathy are more aware of political nuances and how to manage them. This skill becomes increasingly important as you move up the organisational hierarchy. As one CEO inverviewed stated:

> Political savvy is everything at this level and I don't mean being a political animal. I mean being aware of the subtle power plays that are going on when making decisions. Knowing who has the real power and being aware that every move you make will be interpreted as a political gesture. You have got to watch out for that. But being politically manipulative is probably as dangerous as being politically naïve.
>
> CEO, software company

Being politically devious can be detrimental to one's career and the organisation. Political acumen involves knowing who the movers are behind the scenes and always attributing bright ideas to the people who came up with them first. This may seem ethically the only right way but it is also politically discerning. Managers who put forward the ideas of their employees are considered approachable (the employee trusted them enough to approach them with the idea), astute (they recognised a good idea and brought it to the table) and team players (they attributed the idea to the person who made it, not themselves).

Team members who attempt to take the credit for the brainchild of their employees risk destroying their reputation. Political players below them will quickly bypass them and report to someone that they trust to accredit them. The consequence of such an action is merely to look foolish. As one fast tracker stated:

> I quickly realised who to report to and who not to report to. I did not

trust one of my managers and would also go above their head with any ideas I had. The consequence of this was the manager putting forward my idea as her own, the team knowing it was mine, and, a loss of face for the individual in question.

Below is a questionnaire exploring how members of the top team communicate and work together politically. It reflects the typical ways in which you try to persuade others to adopt your view point. The stronger the agreement with each statement, the more one engages in political behaviours in order to persuade or influence.

Table 6.2: How the Top Team Communicate Questionnaire

1 = strongly disagree; 2 = disagree; 3 = neutral; 4 = agree; 5 = strongly agree
— I present rational explanations
— I use persistence and repetition
— I develop the support of important internal or external coalitions
— I offer to trade favours or concessions
— I rely on friendship with other team members
— I build coalitions within the top team
— I present incomplete information about the situation
— I put the most positive spin on the information provided
— I build support for my ideas before meeting the team formally
— I get others inside/outside the team to support my ideas
— I talk behind the scenes with other members in order to persuade them

THE MANAGEMENT OF POWER AND POWER TACTICS

Managing power in an organisation can be like walking a tightrope, surrounded by individuals playing politics and interpreting your behaviour politically. There are many different tactics employed by individuals in order to influence and persuade. See Table 6.3 overleaf.

Table 6.3: Power Tactics

Power Tactics

Reason: use of facts and data – dazzle them with details. This has been found to be the most effective power tactic as it gives the impression of objectivity. The use of this power tactic is not related to hierarchical position, suggesting it is a generic strategy used across various different contexts.[26]

Coalitions: getting support of others to back up request – building up favours so that when support is needed, you will have allies.

Manoeuverability: maintaining flexibility, the avoidance of fully committing to any one idea or depending on any one individual or group.

Negative timing: an executive will often be urged to take action with that which he/she is not in agreement. To give in is undesirable, yet to refuse may be risky. An effective, and much used, tactic is "negative timing". This means initiating but delaying the process of execution – always being in the process of doing something but never quite doing it (citing reasons such as not enough information, need more time, contacts, resources etc). In this way, the executive escapes the charge of evasion, and at the same the undesirable project "dies on the vine".[27]

Control of decision parameters: ensuring the outcome of a decision most benefits you by establishing the criteria against which the acceptability of a solution to a problem is evaluated.

Bargaining: use of negotiation through exchange of benefits or resources. The level you occupy may sometimes affect what resources you have to exchange.

Control of information: where certain information is vital, the less people who have access to it, the more power they possess. Thus, an effective power tactic is to become the sole conduit of certain information.

Control of agendas: controlling the agenda and limiting the number of proposals that appear is a much used power tactic. Under the guise of saving time, committees can be set up to vet the alternatives. Another effective method is to control the order in which items appear, placing unpopular items last or scheduling meetings when opponents are absent.

Impression management: process by which individuals attempt to control the impression others form of them.

Impression management techniques

- Conformity: agreeing with someone to gain their approval.

- Acclaiming: explanation of a favourable event to maximise the desirable implications for oneself or exaggerating role played in a successful project or initiative.

- Flattery: complimenting others about their virtues in an effort to make oneself appear perceptive and likeable. The success of this tactic depends on the individual you are flattering – some individuals are more receptive than others.

> - Association: enhancing or protecting one's image by managing information about people and things with which one is associated.
>
> - Political language: the symbolic use of language in presenting bad news – for example, redundancies become downsizing.

As we mentioned earlier, different top team members will exert varying degrees of power at different times. Certain members of the top team may possess more influence on team decision making than other members. There are different strategies of power use open to these individuals and whichever is used will have repercussions for team effectiveness and social integration. Ruth Wageman's research at Columbia University uncovered three different patterns of power used by top team members at different times to varying degrees of success: overuse, abdication and managing the resource.[28]

Overuse

One pattern of power use identified is that of overuse of the particular source of power. The team member uses the power he or she has in this particular area (client contacts, financial, knowledge based) to exert influence over most aspects of group functioning – even those unrelated to their power source. Such individuals may use their power to control areas beyond their remit. For example, an individual with links to a certain client base may use this to his or her advantage in other areas. Other power sources, for example, status, expertise, knowledge may also be used (or as the case may be, denied) in order to achieve results outside their jurisdiction. The results of such use of power were found to be characterised by widespread dissatisfaction and frustration with both the team itself and the final product as power was used to gain favours, pull strings or force certain decisions in areas outside of the power holders jurisdiction.

Abdication

The second pattern identified was that of abdication. Here the team member does absolutely nothing with his or her potential source of power and exerts no influence over task, internal or external processes. This too was found to be dysfunctional for task effectiveness, corresponding to a laissez-faire style of leadership. This pattern of power use is characterised by a lack of direction and apathy. The power holder fails to use his or her source of power to aid team performance and decision making. Performance was found to be mediocre to poor. However, social relations were found to be positive here as the power holder does not exert his or her influence over the rest of the team.

Managing the resource

Wageman's study found that the most effective pattern was what is termed "managing the resource". In this approach, the emphasis is on managing the areas in which the individual possesses power but not attempting to influence any area outside their remit. Power is used to aid decision making but is not used to influence people/decisions outside the specific area of concern. This was found to be the most effective pattern with these teams performing reasonably well with no particular tendency toward member dissatisfaction.

Thus, the research would suggest that individuals use their power for different ends and that these different uses of power lead to very different consequences for the teams in question. The manipulative political animal leads to member frustration and poor performance and the political non-performer leads to positive group relations but sub-optimal performance. However, individuals who are aware of their power source and use it effectively and appropriately improve the overall performance of the team.

CONCLUSION

Power and politics are inextricably linked to organisational life. The effects on the organisation can be positive or negative depending on the personal motives, the skills and the type of power employed. Different situations require the use of different sources of power. While the era of the knowledge worker means that information, knowledge and expertise are becoming more central as sources of power, this does not detract from the power of the top team and the CEO.

Power games are played on a daily basis – the job of the CEO is not to curb or condone such behaviour but to manage it so that it works to the benefit of the organisation as a whole. This requires an awareness of the tactics used by others to influence, and also the appropriate use of such tactics in achieving organisational ends.

Chapter 7

To Sum Up

INTRODUCTION

We have examined an important set of inter-related factors in this book which impact upon the effective functioning and leadership of the top management team. We now summarise some of the major themes of the book and conclude with some recommendations concerning the complex dilemmas which face those charged with leading the top team and building teamwork at the top.

ASSESSING THE CLIMATE FOR TEAMWORK

One of the first tasks facing the leader of a top team is to consider whether a true team is necessary or possible to create. The leader will also need to gauge the existing climate within an intact top management group and the rapport which exists between the team members. A variety of pressures which mitigate teamwork at the top have been identified including the fact that top teams are frequently composed of ambitious and rivalrous individuals and that the diversity of members' dispositions, values and attitudes engenders conflict within the team. The leadership style displayed by the CEO and the incentive system for top managers may reward individualistic rather than collectivistic behaviour from members of the top management team. Depending on the task complexity and environmental pressures there will be occasions when full teamwork is neither possible nor essential to create.

Katzenbach has identified that true teamwork usually occurs only in top teams faced with a serious environmental threat or internal crisis which jeopardises the survival of the organisational entity itself. It therefore behoves the leader of the top team to consider carefully whether full teamwork is possible. The principle of mutual accountability which accompanies teamwork at the top is a discipline that takes skilful leadership to accomplish but is a very powerful contributor to team effectiveness at this level. It is also important to realise that teamwork is associated with task interdependence and that the careful articulation of a unifying vision plays an essential role in this process.

If the CEO has the luxury of either reconstructing the top management group or selecting an entirely new team, then we recommend that careful attention is paid to the selection of new team members on the basis of likely value added contribution, fit among the various personalities and contribution to balance within the team.

SELECTION OF THE TOP MANAGEMENT TEAM

The importance of composition factors to the effective functioning of the top team cannot be underestimated. Typically, teams are created on a functional basis with little regard to the team role orientation of these members. Each individual member within the team brings a range of values, aptitudes and dispositions to the negotiating arena which characterises the top management group. Typically those who have risen to be functional heads of their respective divisions will have strong personalities. Egocentric behaviour requires subordination within the context of a true team which seeks to balance the need for strategic direction, mutual accountability and consensus decision making.

It is a very useful exercise for the top management group to spend time understanding the motivational base, personality type and team role orientation of each member of the top team. Widely available tools in this regard include Hunt's *Work Interest Schedule*, MBTI and Belbin's *Team Role Orientation*. A frequent reaction of managers who engage in such team assessments is that a greater appreciation and understanding of the factors which irritate them develops, which is frequently associated with a greater acceptance of the other team members. It also has the benefit of creating a shared vocabulary amongst team members.

In constructing the top management team it is important to balance heterogeneity requirements with team "fit". This is because one needs diversity to encourage cognitive conflict within the team which is positive for team effectiveness but which has the potential to spill over into affective/emotionally laden conflict. Team building can be a very useful and effective tool to use in surfacing the latent nature of conflict which may exist between team members and in attempting to "gel" a team to work together on a more trusting basis.

TEAM BUILDING

Team building was identified as focusing on three inter-related domains: purpose, relationships and tasks. Depending on the critical needs of the top management group, team building interventions will focus on one or more of these areas. Purpose-oriented workshops are particularly useful when a team is creating a vision and strategy for the future or when a team is re-assessing its purpose or re-appraising an existing strategy or business plan. It is essential that purpose based workshops are grounded in a realistic and factual assessment of the competitive environment facing the business. Without adequate data, purpose workshops can adopt an air of unreality which quickly translates into a subsequent lack of commitment to the vision and strategy developed. If the top management team is not convinced and committed to a single unifying vision and strategy then the energy and enthusiasm of peers quickly dissipates. The lack of conviction is quickly transmitted throughout the organisation leading to atrophy and despair.

Relationship interventions are a most sensitive area and must be approached with caution. If conflicts are deeply interpersonal in nature a two party intervention between the protagonists facilitated by a skilled team analyst may be more appropriate than a public rehearsal of difference in front of all of the members of the top management group. Team building focusing on task will frequently cut across social relationships amongst team members if these are part of the problem facing the members of the top team.

The openness of the leader of the top team to personal reflection will impact directly upon his or her willingness to engage in team building which involves collective reflection including examination of task and social reflexivity patterns within the top management team. Team building led by a recalcitrant leader is a recipe for failure. Similarly, the leader and team members must be willing to "let go" in team building sessions and must be willing to have flaws and weaknesses exposed.

LEADERSHIP AND SELF-AWARENESS

Another central theme developed in this book has been the need for self-awareness in order that a balanced and effective top team is created. Yet little guidance is given in the literature on how we can become more self-aware. Three levels of self-awareness were identified associated with shallow, moderate and deep self-reflection. Most management development interventions only address the first and perhaps most shallow levels of self-awareness. Typical techniques that can be used here include 360 degree feedback from peers, bosses and subordinates, MBTI and various leadership style self-assessments. To label these as "shallow" does not imply that they lack utility; rather it implies that they only address the surface awareness of participants that their view of the world is frequently very different from that of their peers and colleagues. Moderate level interventions identified include reflection on critical incidents which had a formative influence on an executives behaviour. Deep reflection may involve skilled therapeutic observation of the team members and team leader in action. The surfacing of "undiscussables" through such interventions provides powerful moments of truth for team members. However, time, a precious commodity for teams faced with urgent time pressures, is crucially necessary for such interventions to work.

CONFLICT AT THE TOP

Our discussion of conflict within top management teams has highlighted the positive benefit of conflict as well as some of the well-known negatives. Diversity of background, dispositions and value orientations of team members is an essential element in a successful and effective team. However, it takes skilful management to convert and harness cognitive conflict while minimising the destructive aspects of interpersonal conflict. Tools and techniques which can be used in this regard include negative brainstorming, devil's advocacy, and the motivation and rotation of "critical" roles within the team. We also identified some new approaches to the management of conflict including structured task and social reflexivity assessments as well as team based assessments of members orientations to conflict.

POWER

Power and politics are an inextricable part of organisational life. In our discussion on power, we examined the different reasons for political behaviour including the personality of the individual involved, personal motives, organisational circumstances and the behaviour of others within the organisation. While we do not define power and politics in simplistic terms of legitimate or illegitimate, we do recognise that power deployed for personal gain only can often conflict with the organisational goals. We examined the different sources of power within the organisation and recognised that, while position power is still a central source of power, with flatter organisations and a growing dependence on expertise and knowledge workers, your position in the hierarchy may not reflect your true power. We also discussed the importance of managing power effectively for the CEO – how to empower others while still remaining a leader. Our discussion on power also addressed some of the more practical issues, what political tactics to look out for, what tactics to employ and when to employ these tactics.

TOP MANAGEMENT TEAMS AND THE MANAGEMENT OF PARADOX

In discussing the leadership and management of the top management team a number of paradoxes have been identified. These include the encouragement of both team and non-team behaviours; the creation of dissensus while simultaneously creating high levels of social integration; encouraging cooperation and competition; maintaining the fine grained distinction of mutual dependence, independence and inter-dependence; the need for the team leader to be both close and distant with team members; selecting team members for diversity and also for fit; maintaining a short-term as well as long-term perspective and both an internal and external orientation. Managing the top team is probably best thought of as the management of polarities where polarities can be thought of as mutually interdependent opposites or difficulties which need to be addressed concurrently.[1] The attributes of polarities are that the difficulties are insoluble but can be managed, represent a set of interdependent alternatives, are ongoing, cannot stand alone, the alternatives need each other to optimise the situation over time and always include mutually inclusive opposites.

In concluding, we suggest that careful attention to each of these polarities will pay dividends for top management teams

Encouragement of both non-team and team behaviours within a discipline of mutual accountability

As Katzenbach rightly points out it is important to ensure that "real team discipline or teamwork" is used in appropriate situations.[2] There will be many instances when teams within a team may be helpful to ensure swift action and response to internal and external contingencies. There will be situations where individual responsibility for results to be achieved is the best way forward. Similarly, there will be occasions when collective work opportunities exist which allow the full team to exercise their collective energy and effort to maximise team performance. These occasions are valuable, as the process of collective work will assist in the creation of a cohesive team derived from goal attainment. One discipline, however, remains paramount. This is the principle of mutual accountability for the achievement of agreed targets.

Encouraging cognitive conflict to minimise group-think while encouraging a climate of supportive and cooperative team behaviours

This is one of the most difficult balancing acts to achieve and requires both skilful team leadership and the practice of structured techniques such as devil's advocacy and the stepladder technique outlined earlier. The use of trainers to coach the team in such techniques can be extremely valuable. Top management teams need to train hard to use the sporting analogy and part of the training regime should include guidance in the use of such techniques.

Encouraging cooperation and competition within the top management group

Senior managers need to be challenged at a personal level in order to maximise team performance. The skilful team leader will need to appraise when his or her functional direct reports should be encouraged to compete with each other to boost operating unit performance and when they should be encouraged to cooperate to maximise team performance and organisational performance. Not all management groups can or will want to get along with each other unless careful attention has been paid to the issue of balance within the team. Balance within the team, as we have seen, involves assessing the mix of personalities, egos and team role orientations as well as the knowledge, skills, abilities and networks of the various team members.

Balancing independence, interdependence and dependency relationships within the team

This is a critical "trip wire" to manage. Members of the top management group are usually independent critical thinkers. They also represent constituencies of interest within the organisation. In a top performing team the leader must ensure that the "general management point of view" prevails which ensures that the collective welfare of the organisation is maximised for the various stakeholders involved. To ensure that the collective benefit for all members is maximised implies that mutual dependence needs to be acknowledged amongst strong-minded individuals. True awareness of our interdependence occurs when we realise that we depend on others to support us in our activities.

CEO as leader and servant

To lead successfully as a transformational leader involves the willingness to empower others to make decisions and to provide a context for decentralisation within the organisation. To demonstrate true empowerment, large domains of influence must be delegated which may once have been the sole province of the CEO. This requires trusting the top team and the organisation as a whole. What is important here is that empowerment is not just seen as an empty gesture or as the "emperor's new clothes"[3] – promises to delegate power must be backed up with realistic steps to put this in action. Letting go can be difficult, especially if certain decisions might affect the bottom line. However, the alternative – empowering people only to detract power when the decision is important – will only demotivate people and engender distrust. The effective leader equips followers with the skills and confidence to make certain decisions and then follows through by encouraging them and empowering them to make these decisions.

Selecting team members for diversity and for "fit"

Another critical dilemma for the CEO is to ensure that the top team achieves balance in the mix of personalities, egos and team role orientations as well as the knowledge skills, abilities and networks of the various team members. The context in which the team works will also greatly determine the appropriate mix. For example, when working within an ever-changing, highly technological and competitive environment, a highly analytical team would not be suitable. While the correct "fit" is crucial, it is also important to ensure that there is the right amount of diversity within the top team. A team that is composed of individuals who are similar in personality, values and team role orientations often fall prey to group-think. In order to prevent this, and to stimulate creativity and innovation, a certain amount of diversity within the team balanced with the appropriate "fit" is essential.

Maintain a short-term and long-term orientation

The team must have a sense of short-term goals to be achieved within the context of a long-term strategy and vision. Too much focus on one without the other will lead to an under performing team. Yet there is a tendency to yield to short termism in decision making which can be destructive when long-term goals are sacrificed in the process. While it is necessary to keep an eye on operational issues on a day to day basis, it is also necessary to fit daily decisions and their implications into the wider strategic context.

Foster an internal and external orientation

A team which does not have a strong balance of external and internal networks risks a lack of information on new ideas, new ways of solving existing problems and the capacity to implement strategy. It is crucially important to maintain links to the outside environment represented by customers, suppliers and venture capital in order to ensure a strong stream of new product innovations are developed. Similarly, it is important to cultivate a strong network internally in order to ensure that intended strategy is in fact realised. An effective leader will successfully manage this balancing act between internal and external needs and constraints.

CONCLUSION

We believe that the new challenge for today's leader is to successfully manage the many polarities facing the CEO and top team. This requires a tolerance for ambiguity and uncertainty, a "balanced" team, an awareness of one's strengths and weaknesses, and the compensation for the latter, the encouragement of cognitive conflict and a dedication to fostering an environment of trust and openness within the team. We hope this book goes some of the way towards helping you, the reader, to address these challenges.

Notes to Chapters

Chapter One

1. Hambrick, D. 1994. Top Management Groups: A Conceptual Integration and Reconsideration of the Label "Team". *Research in Organisational Behaviour*, 16:171-213.
2. Finkelstein, S. 1992. Power in Top Management Teams: Dimensions, Measurement and Validation. *Academy of Management Journal*, 35:505-538; Hambrick, D. 1994. Top Management Groups: A Conceptual Integration and Reconsideration of the Label "Team". *Research in Organisational Behaviour*, 16:171-213; Bourgeois, L. J. III. 1980. Performance and Consensus. *Strategic Management Journal*, 1:227-248; Hambrick, D. and Mason, P. A. 1984. Upper Echelons: The Organisation as a Reflection of its Top Managers. *Academy of Management Review*, 9:195-206.
3. See Finkelstein, S. and Hambrick, D. 1996. *Strategic Leadership: Top Executives and their Effects on Organisations*. West Publishing Company; Flood, P., Fong, C. M., Smith, K. G., O'Regan, P., Moore, S. and Morley, M. 1997. Pioneering in Top Management Teams: A Resource Based Perspective. *International Journal of Human Resource Management*, 8(3):291–303.
4. Hage, J. and Dewar, R. 1973. Elite Values Versus Organisational Structure in Predicting Innovations. *Administrative Science Quarterly*, 18:279-290 (as cited in Finkelstein, S. and Hambrick, D. 1996. *Strategic Leadership: Top Executives and their Effects on Organisations*. West Publishing Company).
5. Halebian, J. and Finkelstein, S. 1993. Top Management Team Size, CEO Dominance, and Firm Performance: The Moderating Roles of the Environmental Turbulence and Discretion. *Academy of Management Journal*, 36:844-863 (as cited in Finkelstein, S. and Hambrick, D. 1996. *Strategic Leadership: Top Executives and their Effects on Organisations*. West Publishing Company).
6. West, M. A. 1994. *Effective Teamwork*. BPS Books.
7. Finkelstein, S. and Hambrick, D. 1996. *Strategic Leadership: Top Executives and their Effects on Organisations*. West Publishing Company.
8. Katzenbach, J. R. 1997. The Myth of the Top Management Team. *Harvard Business Review*, Nov-Dec, 83-91.
9. Hambrick, D. 1994. Top Management Groups: A Conceptual Integration and Reconsideration of the Label "Team". *Research in Organisational Behaviour*, 16:171-213.
10. Finkelstein, S. and Hambrick, D. 1996. *Strategic Leadership: Top Executives and their Effects on Organisations*. West Publishing Company.
11. Hambrick, D. 1994. Top Management Groups: A Conceptual Integration and Reconsideration of the Label "Team". *Research in Organisational Behaviour*, 16:171-213.

12. Katzenbach, J. R. 1997. The Myth of the Top Management Team. *Harvard Business Review*, Nov-Dec, 83-91.
13. Allaire, P. 1998. Lessons in Teamwork. *Navigating Change: How CEOs, Top Teams and Boards Steer Transformation*, eds D. Hambrick, D. A. Nadler and M. L. Tushman. The Management of Innovation and Change Series. Harvard.
14. Vancil, R. F. 1987. *Passing the Baton*. Harvard Business School Press.
15. Finkelstein, S. and Hambrick, D. 1996. *Strategic Leadership: Top Executives and their Effects on Organisations*. West Publishing Company.
16. Eisenhardt, K. M. and Bourgeois, L. J. 1988. Politics of Strategic Decision Making in High Velocity Environments: Toward a Midrange Theory. *Academy of Management Journal*, 32:543-76.
17. Finkelstein, S. 1992. Power in Top Management Teams: Dimensions, Measurement and Validation. *Academy of Management Journal*, 35:505-538.
18. Hambrick, D. 1987. Top Management Teams: Key to Strategic Success. *California Management Review*, 30:88-108.
19. Keck, S. L. and Tushman, M. L. 1992. Environmental and organisational context and Executive Team Structure. *Academy of Management Journal*, 36:1314-1344.
20. Hambrick, D. 1994. Top Management Groups: A Conceptual Integration and Reconsideration of the Label "Team". *Research in Organisational Behaviour*, 16:171-213.
21. Hambrick, D. 1981. Environment, Strategy, and Power within Top Management Teams. *Administrative Science Quarterly*, 26:253-276.
22. Miles, R. and Snow, C. 1978. *Organisational Strategy, Structure and Process*. McGraw Hill.
23. Starbuck, W., Greve A. and Hedberg, B. L. T. 1978. Responding to Crisis. *Journal of Business Administration*, 9:111-137.
24. Staw, B. M., Sandelands, L. E. and Dutton, J. E. 1981. Threat Rigidity Effects in Organisational Behaviour: A Multi Level Analysis. *Administration Science Quarterly*, 26:501-524.
25. Smith, K. G., Smith, K. A., Olian, J. and Sims, H. Teamwork at the Top: Management Influence on Strategy and Performance. A Management Study by Maryland Business School Faculty, unpublished mimeograph.
26. O'Reilly C. A. and Flatt, S. 1989. Executive Team Demography, Organisational Innovation and Firm Performance. Working paper, University of Calafornia, Berkeley.
27. Ancona, D. G. and Caldwell, D. F. 1992. Bridging the Boundary: External Activity and Performance in Organisational Teams. *Administrative Science Quarterly*, 37:634-665.
28. Smith, K. G., Smith, K. A., Olian, J. and Sims, H. Teamwork at the Top: Management Influence on Strategy and Performance. A Management Study by Maryland Business School Faculty, unpublished mimeograph.
29. Jackson, S. E. 1992. Consequences of Group Composition for the Interpersonal Dynamics of Strategic Issue Processing. *Advances in Strategic Management*, eds P. Shrivastava, A. Huff and J. Dutton, 8: 345-382. JAI Press.
30. Schweiger, D. M., Sandberg, W. R. and Rechner, P. L. 1989. Experiential Effects of Dialectic Inquiry, Devil's Advocacy and Consensus Approaches to Strategic Decision Making. *Academy of Management Journal*, 32:745-772.
31. Eisenhardt, K. and Bourgeois, L. J. 1988. Politics of Strategic Decision Making

in High Velocity Environments: Towards a Mid Range Theory. *Academy of Management Journal*, 31:737-770.

32. Weick, K. E. 1969. *The Social Psychology of Organising*. Addison-Wesley.

Chapter Two

1. Anacona, D. G. and Nadler, D. A. 1989. Top Hats and Executive Tales: Designing the Senior Team. *Sloan Management Review*, fall, 19-28.
2. Hambrick, D. 1987. Top Management Teams: Key to Strategic Success. *California Management Review*, 30:88-108.
3. Finkelstein, S. and Hambrick, D. 1996. *Strategic Leadership: Top Executives and their Effects on Organisations*. West Publishing Company.
4. Hambrick D. and Brandon, G. 1988. Executive Values. *The Executive Effect: Concepts and Methods for Studying Top Managers*, ed. D. Hambrick, 3-34. JAI Press. They consolidated the five value schemes of Allport, G. W.,Vernon P. E. and Lindzey, G. 1970. *Study of Values*. Houghton Mifflin; Rokeach, M. 1973. *The Nature of Human Values*. Free Press; England, G. W. 1967. Personal Values Systems of American Managers. *Academy of Management Journal*, 10: 53-68 and Hofstede, G. 1980. *Culture's Consequences: International Differences in Work Related Values*. Sage.
5. Cohen, A. R. and Bradford, D. L. 1989. Influence Without Authority: The Use of Alliances, Reciprocity and Exchange to Accomplish Work. *Organisational Dynamics*, 17(3):4-18.
6. Hambrick, D. 1987. Top Management Teams: Key to Strategic Success. *California Management Review*, 30:88-108.
7. Katzenbach, J. R. 1997. The Myth of the Top Management Team. *Harvard Business Review*, Nov-Dec, 83-91.
8. Myers, I. B. 1982. *Introduction to Type*. Consulting Psychologists Press.
9. Jung, C. 1921. *Psychological Types*. Routledge.
10. Buchanan, D. and Huczynski, A. 1997. *Organisational Behaviour: An Introductory Text*. Prentice Hall.
11. Senior, B. 1997. Team Roles and Team Performance: Is There "Really" a Link? *Journal of Occupational and Organisational Psychology*, Sept, 70(3): 241-59 based on Belbin, 1993, 100-101.
12. Belbin, R. M. 1996. *The Coming Shape of Organisation*. Butterworth Heinemann.
13. Buchanan, D. and Huczynski, A. 1997. *Organisational Behaviour: An Introductory Text*. Prentice Hall.
14. Katzenbach, J. R. and Smith, D. K. 1993. *The Wisdom of Teams: Creating the High Performance Organisation*. Harvard Business School Press.
15. Senior, B. 1997. Team Roles and Team Performance: Is There "Really" a Link? *Journal of Occupational and Organisational Psychology*, 70(3): 241-59 based on Belbin, 1993, 100-101.
16. Galpin, T. 1994. How to Manage Human Performance. *Employment Relations Today*, summer, 207-225.
17. Shi, Y. and Tang, H. K. 1997. Team Role Behaviour and Task Environment: An Exploratory Study of Five Organisations and Their Manager. *Journal of Managerial Psychology*, Jan-Feb, 12(1-2): 85-95.

18. Finkelstein, S. and Hambrick, D. 1996. *Strategic Leadership: Top Executives and their Effects on Organisations.* West Publishing Company.
19. Finkelstein, S. 1992. Power in Top Management Teams: Dimensions, Measurements and Validations. *Academy of Management Journal*, 35:505-538, as cited in Finkelstein, S. and Hambrick, D. 1996. *Strategic Leadership: Top Executives and their Effects on Organisations.* West Publishing Company.
20. Amason, A. C. 1996. Distinguishing the Effects of Functional and Dysfunctional Conflict on Strategic Decision Making: Resolving a Paradox for Top Management Teams. *Academy of Management Journal*, Feb, 39(1):123-149.
21. Knight, D., Pearce, C., Smith, K. G., Olian, J. D., Sims, H. P., Smith, K. A. and Flood, P. 1999. Top Management Team Diversity, Group Processes and Strategic Consensus. *Strategic Managment Journal*, 20: 445-465.
22. Hurst, D. K., Rush J. C.and White R. E. 1989. Top Management Teams and Organisational Renewal. *Strategic Management Journal*, 10 (Special Issue):87-105.

Chapter Three

1. Woodcock, M. and Francis, D. 1994. *Team Building Strategy*. 2nd edition. Gower.
2. *Ibid.*
3. Stoner, C. and Hartman, R. 1993. Team Building: Answering the Tough Questions. *Business Horizons*, Sept-Oct, 36(5):70-79.
4. Buck, J. T. 1995. The Rocky Road to Team-based Management. *Training and Development*, April, 35-38.
5. Stoner, C. and Hartman, R. 1993. Team Building: Answering the Tough Questions. *Business Horizons*, Sept-Oct, 36(5):70-79.
6. Heap, N. 1996. Building the Organisational Team. *Industrial and Commercial Training*, 28(3): 3-7.
7. Adapted from Nilson, C. 1992. *Team Games for Trainers*. McGraw Hill.
8. Jaffe, D. T and Scott, C. D. 1998. How to Link Personal Values with Team Values. *Training and Development,* March, 52(3):25-30.
9. Critchley, B. and Casey, D. 1996. Second Thoughts on Team Building. *How Organisations Learn*, ed. K. Starkey. Thomson Business Press.
10. Robbins, D. 1993. The Dark Side of Team Building. *Training and Development*, Dec, 47(12):17-22.

Chapter Four

1. Scully, J. A., Sims, H. P., Olian, J. D., Schnell, E. R. and Smith, K.A. 1994. Tough Times Make Tough Bosses: A Meso Analysis of CEO Leadership Behaviour. *Leadership Quarterly*, 15(1):59-83.
2. Hambrick, D. and D'Aveni, R. 1992. Top Team Deterioration as Part of the Downward Spiral of Large Corporate Bankruptcies. *Management Science*, 38:1445-1466.
3. Bass, B. M. 1985. *Leadership and Performance Beyond Expectations*. Free Press.
4. *Ibid.*, 31.
5. Kets de Vries, M. 1998. Charisma in Action: The Transformational Abilities of

Virgin's Richard Branson and ABB's Percy Barnevik. *Organisational Dynamics*, winter, 26(3): 6-22.

6. Tichy, N. M. and Devanna, M. A. 1986. *The Transformational Leader.* John Wiley & Sons.

7. Argyris, C. 1986. Skilled Incompetence. *Harvard Business Review*, Sept-Oct, 74-79.

8. Tichy, N. M. and Devanna, M. A. 1986. *The Transformational Leader.* John Wiley & Sons.

9. Larry Ellison being interviewed on the BBC.

10. Goleman, D. 1998. *Working with Emotional Intelligence.* Bloomsbury

11. Bennis, W. 1997. *Why Leaders Can't Lead: The Unconscious Conspiracy Continues.* Jossey Bass.

12. Hunt, J. and Laing, B. 1997. Leadership: The Role of the Exemplar. *Business Strategy Review*, spring, 8(1): 31-43.

13. Cooper and Sawaf, 1997. *Executive EQ: Emotional Intelligence in Business.* Orion Business Books.

14. Boyett, J. and Boyett, J. 1998. *The Guru Guide: The Best Ideas of Top Management Thinkers*, 7. John Wiley & Sons.

15. Quote taken from Dess, G. D. and Picken, J. C. 2000. Changing Roles: Leadership in the 21st Century. *Organisational Dynamics,* winter, 18-33.

16. Rao, A., Schmidt, S. M. and Murray, L. H. 1995. Upward Impression Management: Goals, Influence, Strategies and Consequences. *Human Relations*, Feb, 48(2):147-168.

17. Martin, D. 1998. Impression Management, http://www.nwmissouri.edu/nwcourses/martin/socialpsych/impmanag/sldoo1.htm

18. Study conducted by the University of Limerick and University of Maryland on Top Management teams, 1994-1998 directed by Patrick Flood and Ken G. Smith.

19. Smith, K. G., Smith, K. A., Olian, J. D., Sims, H. P., O'Bannon, D. P. and Scully, J. A. 1994. Top management Team Demography and Process: The Role of Social Integration and Communication. *Administrative Science Quarterly*, 39:412-438. See also, Flood, P., Hannan, E., Smith, K.G., Turner, T., West, M. and Dawson, J. 2000. Chief Executive Leadership Style, Consensus Decisions Making, and Top Management Team Effectiveness. *European Journal of Work and Organisational Psychology*, 9(3):401-420.

20. Yukl, G. 1998. *Leadership in Organisations.* 4th edition. Prentice Hall.

21. Eisenhardt, K. M. 1989. Making Fast Decisions in High Velocity Environments. *Academy of Management Journal*, 32:543-576.

22. Goffee, R. and Jones, G. 1998. The Character of a Corporation: How your Company's Culture can Make or Break your Business. Harper Collins.

23. Tichy, N. M. and Sherman, S. 1994. *Control Your Own Destiny or Someone Else Will*, Harper Business.

24. Yukl, G. 1998. *Leadership in Organisations.* 4th edition. Prentice Hall.

25. Nadler D. A. and Heilpern, J. D. 1998. The CEO in the Context of Discontinuous Change. *Navigating Change: How CEOs, Top Teams and Boards Steer Transformation*, eds D. Hambrick, D. A. Nadler and M. L. Tushman. The Management of Innovation and Change Series. Harvard.

26. Yukl, G. 1998. *Leadership in Organisations.* 4th edition. Prentice Hall.

27. Hunt, J. 1997. *Managing People at Work.* McGraw Hill.

28. *Ibid.*
29. Quote taken from Dess, G. D. and Picken, J. C. 2000. Changing Roles: Leadership in the 21st Century. *Organisational Dynamics,* winter, 18-33.
30. *Ibid.*
31. Argyris, C. 1986. Skilled Incompetence. *Harvard Business Review*, Sept-Oct, 74-79.
32. *Ibid.*

Chapter Five

1. Murrow, E., American journalist in 1950's speech on democracy and change.
2. Hambrick, D. 1995. Fragmentation and the Other Problems CEOs have with their Top Management Teams. *California Management Review*, 37(3):111-127.
3. Katz, R. 1982. The Effects of Group Longevity on Project Communication and Performance. *Administrative Science Quarterly,* 27:81-104.
4. Jehn, K. 1997. A Qualitiative Analysis of Conflict Types and Dimensions in Organisational Groups. *Administrative Science Quarterly*, 42:530-557.
5. Amason, A. C. 1996. Distinguishing between the Effects of Functional and Dysfunctional Conflict on Strategic Decision Making: Resolving a Paradox for Top Management Teams. *Academy of Management Journal*, 39(1):123-149.
6. Hannan, E. 1998. *CEO Leadership and Teams at the Top: Impact of CEO Leadership Styles on Group Processes, Team Effectiveness and Firm Performance*, MSc dissertation in Occupational Psychology, Institute of Work Psychology, University of Sheffield.
7. Simons, T. L. and Peterson, R. S. 2000. Task Conflict and Relationship Conflict in Top Managment Teams: The Pivotal Role of Intragroup Trust, *Journal of Applied Psychology*, 85(1):102-111.
8. Dess, G. D. and Picken, J. C. 2000. Changing Roles: Leadership in the 21st Century. *Organisational Dynamics*, winter,18-33.
9. Eisenhardt, K. M., Kahwajy, J. and Bourgeois, L. J. III, 1997. Conflict and Strategic Choice: How Top Management Teams Disagree. *California Management Review*, 39(2):42-55.
10. Jehn, K. 1997. A Qualitiative Analysis of Conflict Types and Dimensions in Organisational Groups. *Administrative Science Quarterly*, 42:530-557.
11. *Ibid.*; Jehn, K. 1995. A Multimethod Examination of the Benefits and Detriments of Intragroup Conflict. *Administrative Science Quarterly*, 40(2):256-283.
12. Thomas-Kilmann Conflict Mode Instrument, written by Kenneth Thomas and Ralph Kilmann and published by Xicom.
13. Jehn, K. 1995. A Multimethod Examination of the Benefits and Detriments of Intragroup Conflict. *Administrative Science Quarterly*, 40(2):256-283.
14. Mischel, W. 1977. The Interaction of Person and Situation. Personality at the Crossroads: Current Issues in Interactional Pyschology, eds D. Magnusson and Endler, N. S., 333-352.
15. O'Donnell, D. and Flood, P. 1999. The Emotional World of Strategy Implementation. Paper presented to Eastern Academy of Management Conference, Managing in a Global Economy VIII, Prague, June, 20-24.

Chapter Six

1. Nietzsche, F. 1968. *The Will to Power*, trans. W. Kaufmann and R. J. Hothingdale. Vintage Books.
2. Hannan, E. 1998. *CEO Leadership and Teams at the Top*. MSC in Occupational Psychology.
3. French, J. R. P. Jr and Raven, B. 1959. The Bases of Social Power. *Studies in Social Power*, ed. D. Cartwright.
4. Finkelstein, S. 1992. Power in Top Management Teams: Dimensions, Measurement and Validation. *Academy of Management Journal*, Aug, 35(3):505-537.
5. *Ibid.*
6. *Ibid.*
7. Tichy, N. M. and Devanna, M. A. 1986. *The Transformational Leader*. John Wiley & Sons.
8. Mintzberg, H. 1983. *Power in and around Organisations*. Prentice Hall.
9. Buchanan, D. and Badham, R. 1999. Politics and Organisational Change: The Lived Experience. *Human Relations*, 52(5):609.
10. *Ibid.*
11. Brass, D. J. 1984. Being in the Right Place: A Structural Analysis of Individual Influence in and around Organisations. *Administrative Science Quarterly*, 29:518-539 and Galaskiewicz, J. 1979. *Exchange Networks and Community Politics*. Sage.
12. Martin, N. H. and Sims, J. H. 1956. The Exercise of Power in Organisations. *Harvard Business Review*, Nov-Dec, 25-29.
13. Tichy, N. M. and Devanna, M. A. 1986. *The Transformational Leader*. John Wiley & Sons.
14. Quote taken from Smith, S. B. 1990. In all his Glory: The Life of William S. Paley. Simon & Schuster as cited in Pfetter, J. 1992. *Managing with Power: Politics and Influences in Organisations*. Harvard Business School Press.
15. Clark, K., Smith, K. G., Sims, H. P., Flood, P., Moore, S., Morley, M. and O'Regan, P. 1997. Configuration of Top Management Teams: Structure, Composition, Process, Power and Leadership. Paper presented at the Organisational and Management Theory Division of the Academy of Management at the annual meeting in Boston.
16. *Ibid.*, 26.
17. *Ibid.*, 19.
18. Meyer, J. M. and Rowan, B. 1977. Institutionalised Organisation: Formal Structures as Myth and Ceremony. *American Journal of Sociology*, 83(2):340-363.
19. McClelland, D. C., Atkinson, J. W., Clark, R. A. and Lowell, E. L. 1958. A Scoring Manual for the Achievement Motive. *Motives in Fantasy, Action and Society*, ed. John W. Atkinson, 179-204. Van Nostrand.
20. McClelland, D. C. and Boyatzis, D. 1982. Leadership Motive Pattern and Long Term Success in Management. *Journal of Applied Psychology*, 67:737-743.
21. House, R. 1977. A 1976. Theory of Charismatic Leadership. *Leadership: The Cutting Edge*, eds J. G. Hunt and L. L. Larson, 189-207. Southern Illinois University Press.
22. Kets DeVries, M. F. R. 1994. *Organisational Paradoxes: Clinical Approaches to Management*. 2nd edition. Routledge.

23. *Ibid.*
24. As cited in Forsberg, M. 1993. Childhood Affects Office Politics, Personnel Journal, 72(8):29-33.
25. Kets DeVries, M. F. R. 1994. *Organisational Paradoxes: Clinical Approaches to Management.* 2nd edition. Routledge.
26. Brass, D. J. and Burkhardt, M. E. 1993. Political Power and Power Use: An Investigation of Structure and Behaviour. *Academy of Management Journal,* 36(3):441-471.
27. Martin, N. H. and Sims, J. H. 1956. The Exercise of Power in Organisations. *Harvard Business Review*, Nov-Dec, 25-29.
28. Wageman, R. and Mannix, E. 1998. Uses and Misuses of Power in Task-performing Teams. *Power and Influence in Organisations*, eds Kramer, R. and Neale, M. Sage.

Chapter Seven

1. Dromgoole, T. and Mullins, D. Strategy Implementation and Polarity Management. 2000. *Managing Strategy Implementation*, eds Flood, P., Dromgoole, T., Carroll, S. and Gorman, L. Blackwell.
2. Katzenbach, J. R., 1997. The Myth of the Top Management Team. *Harvard Business Review*, Nov-Dec, 83-91.
3. A term applied by Chris Argyris to the case of empowerment.

Index of Names

Index

IRISH MANAGEMENT INSTITUTE

The Irish Management Institute is a not-for-profit membership organisation at the forefront of management and organisational development in Ireland. It works with individuals and organisations to improve performance through excellence in the practice of management. The IMI has built an international reputation in the field of adult learning and through its work, contributes to Irish economic and social development. The IMI provides management training and development for more than 4500 individual managers every year. Through our conferences, regional structures and programmes, we provide a forum for our members to exchange experience, access international expertise and develop leading edge management practice.

Irish Management Institute,
National Management Centre,
Sandyford Road,
Dublin 16,
Ireland.
Telephone: 353 1 207 8400
Fax: 353 1 295 5150
Email: reception@imi.ie
Website: www.imi.ie